8-17-2016

HOWARD PARKER !!!

A Long Time Brother + Friend
God BLESS You Howard !!!

MY BRIDGE OVER TROUBLED WATERS

Wesley Hawkins Jr.

RESPECT + LOVE

MY BRIDGE OVER TROUBLED WATERS
by Wesley Hawkins Jr.

Printed in the United States of America

ISBN 9781629526478

www.xulonpress.com

Introduction

This book is based on a true life experience of a native of Atlantic City, New Jersey, a former Police Officer of Atlantic City Police Department, member of Omega Psi Phi Fraternity, Inc., single father of three children that I raised through the power of Jesus Christ. On October 14th, 1981, in the early morning hours, it all began, twist and turns in the world of life for me. Again stepping out on faith, from the incident shoot-out on top of the Albany Avenue Bridge, in which my partner paid the uttermost sacrifice, his life; he was driving and I sat next to him, not realizing nor having any control of the pursuit we were involved with. Death was knocking at my door. It surrounded me three times in a twenty second period. "My partner" at the time of his death was only twenty years old.

Again "stepping out", resigning from being a community law-enforcement officer with the A.C.P.D., I kept holding on to my faith and belief, not realizing Jesus and his Father had a plan. But, I had to go through some changes in my journey through life, staying focused on my Savior!

Approximately 30 plus years later, I now conclude "My Bridge Troubled Waters":

"My Bridge Over Troubled Waters!"

Wesley Hawkins, Jr.

2014

Copyright

My sole intention is to show no matter how the cards of life are dealt to you, you must keep your faith, believe, and hold on to Jesus! "He can do all things. . .all things. . . but fail". No matter when Jesus arrives to your situation, He's going to be right on time!

I give Him, "ALL THE PRAISE!"

Wesley Hawkins, Jr.

2014

Dedication

From the desktop of Author, Wesley Hawkins, Jr. I Welcome all to my testimony, which has taken some years to come to fruition! I have learned I can't move on my time; rather it best to move with His!

I give all, all praises to my Lord and Savior, Jesus, the Christ! Jesus was standing with me when I thought I was alone. Jesus had me the whole time. . . Now, we have each other! None of us is perfect like our Jesus; we all fall short of Him. I, like most others, am a work in progress! Most may feel that Jesus may not be there when we want Him, but keep your faith and trust in Him. . . When Jesus steps into your situation, He is right on time!

In Memory of my Mother, and total appreciation of my Dad, for both of them giving me understanding, direction, and most of all, support from the mistreatment of the office of Public Safety! (particularly) the Atlantic City Police Department, where my Dad and I put our lives on the line, in near death situations that happened while employed as Police Officers for the City of Atlantic City!

All police officers, in this country take an oath to "Protect and Serve" under the Constitution, its citizens and visitors alike!

Law enforcement officers, I'm quite sure, there is a message in my book for you. Only you will be able to make that decision!

My Grandmother, a single parent, who raised seven children. She is in Glory, with two of her daughters - my mom, and her oldest daughter, Betty. I learned from my Grandmother, she knew just what it took to be a single parent, a responsibility for your children! Having structure, value and education were her goals for her children and grandchildren!

My Fraternity, Omega Psi Phi Fraternity, Inc.! Most of my Brothers whom I have met during my journey through life "stepping" along the way, some others have passed on to Omega Chapter. That mighty Royal Purple and Old Gold have been planted deep, deep within my soul! Bruhz, you know and I know, who you are! Thanks so very much Team, with all your support, in the pain that I may have expressed, with the frustration, because of what was on my plate! Taking out some time to hear me vent, I thank you! We all fall short, again no one is perfect, to our Lord and Savior! But. . . "Friendship is essential to the soul!"

The Women, at my church, Second Baptist Church, on my job (City-Welfare) and those ladies who knew of my circumstances at home. They all had a common denominator. . . they loved the Lord and reached out to others, (helping) in the name of Jesus! My children's biological mother was not present or had any contact with them at such early ages, on a daily, weekly, monthly or yearly basis, but it was, what it was, and I chose to deal with it! And I, did! My daughter, the youngest and only girl of the three males including me in our home! Wow, these ladies (in different stages of her life) were a blessing for all of us!

Yes, I have a sister and other female family members that spent money and time on special occasions with my daughter in her rearing! One thing is for sure, she has made me proud, very proud over the years in growing up!

Miriah seems to keep Jesus close to her heart and mind! She is very mature for her age and responsible to herself! I realize children will be children and they must find their way! We all have free choice, it was given to us by our Lord and Savior! I will always, always be Dad to all my children; that is my responsibility to them!

I stated at Bible Study one Wednesday night, that I stepped out again, the first time, (10/14/81) with a shot-gun, pulling the trigger! The second time, (8/18/1988) resigning from the Police Department. I was still holding on to my faith and having the belief that no harm would ever put me under! The adversary or Satan will try to get a grip on your life, but when you are washed in the blood and put yourself with the Lord's favor, you will be under constant attack! Remember, "Jesus can do all things, but fail!"

Finally, I don't know what will happen to us a people! I survived to the utmost, an extremely violent incident in law enforcement! (10/14/81) My Partner paid the ultimate sacrifice, his life!

Some thirty plus years later, I don't know what's in store for us as a free society! Guns, everyone seems to have one, and they are using them! Legal or not, guns kill! No more Saturday night specials or small caliber guns, (22) on the streets of America. One large caliber gun took out my partner, although found in the trunk of the suspect's vehicle was a high powered rifle and ammunition for the many weapons he had in his possession! The real kick to me was the suspect was discharged from the military for being a sexual pervert towards a child! What was he doing, having legal possession? Sounds like a mental disorder on both sides of the fence! We must tighten the laws on these guns and owners! What kind of incident will it take, involving guns for us to focus on changing the laws for our safety in this country? We must revisit the "Right to Bear Arms" and get these guns and clips for high power assault weapons from those that are in our society. They pose a threat for mass killings in the streets. Schools, malls, and movie theaters where ever people may gather! It's just a matter of time, for us as a country to wish we had done something much earlier to avoid a mass murder involving high powered guns!

We all take falls in our lives, but we can't just lay there when we are down! Someone, who sits high, looks & reaches down low will pull you up and out of your situations. You can trust and believe! If I had never trusted the Lord, I would've been stuck on this island! Why? I would be too afraid to cross over a bridge, because of my incident! I would've been stuck in Atlantic City, New Jersey, never to have traveled beyond!

Therefore, you must trust and believe that any obstacle in your life can be overcome. I now present, "My Bridge Over Troubled Waters!"

RESPECTFULLY

WESLEY HAWKINS JR

2014

Table of Content

Chapter One

"In The Beginning"

I was born on December 12, 1956 to Wesley and Grace Hawkins. I am their only son. I have a sister, who is about two years older. We lived in public housing, Stanley Holmes Village, on City Place located in the first village. As a youngster, I remember some of our neighbors. They watched my sister and me or gave us treats such as homemade cookies, a slice of cake, or pie! My favorite treat was homemade mashed potatoes with butter. I later learned most of the men who lived in Stanley Holmes Village were war veterans holding down some type of government employment. Policemen, Firemen, and Mailmen, a working class of men taking on the responsibility of their family. One of the men was a former mayor of Pleasantville, New Jersey, and an Atlantic County sheriff officer, decades down the road became an under-sheriff and a well-known police detective, was the first of his ethnicity to be made detective, who is now deceased. All were well known to their families and the communities where they lived and served.

Within six years of my birth, my parents purchased a home. I believe this was also after the Hurricane of March 1962! The home was located in the Bungalow Park, uptown section of the city. It was a black and white two story duplex. My family lived upstairs and my parents rented the downstairs out to working individuals or some families during my younger years.

I started kindergarten in 1963, at New Jersey Avenue School. The school was located approximately six blocks from our residence. The staff, teachers, and principals were great people for the most part. Some teachers were involved in activities such as scouting, bike riding on Saturday's along the Boardwalk or bowling parties at Boardwalk Bowl located Arkansas and the Boardwalk just to name a few activities I was involved in while attending New Jersey Avenue School. During this time Atlantic City had two middle schools, better known by some as Junior High School. This was seventh and eighth grade, which prepared you for high school. This involved changing classes, using buses or Jitneys for public transportation, and walking through the city to pursue an education. I attended Central Junior High located at the corner of Ohio and Pacific Avenue.

The other middle school was located on the corner of Texas and Arctic Avenues; its name was Chelsea Junior High. If you attended *Central Junior High, you would graduate from high school not being left back, on an odd year, Chelsea* Junior High the opposite an even year. I went to Central Junior High in the seventh grade only. The eighth grade I had my learning disabilities and behavior issues like most teenagers, but my parents expected more from me, and I had to deliver, because I had the help of Jesus, and he doesn't fail.

September 1970, I attended Stratford Military Academy in Stratford, New Jersey. It was an all-male, mix races and cultures, strongly disciplined, boarding school. You had to carry all your books in your book bag, during classes, study hall, weeknights and weekends. It was said, and I believe "if you carry your books now, your books will carry you throughout life". I brought my learning level in reading, writing, math and English, from fourth and fifth grade level to tenth grade level in the one year that I attended Stratford. Also every word when speaking to an adult ended with "Yes mama" or "Yes sir" or the opposite. I promised my parents, if they allowed me to attend Atlantic City High School (A.C.H.S.), the following school year, because Stratford only went up to the eighth grade. Yes, I was a proud high school bound cadet in which I did graduate! My parents' decisions were made to grant me approval to return as a freshman at Atlantic City High School, home of the Vikings, September of 1971.

I was familiar with some of the other freshmen from Central Junior High, attending A.C.H.S. We were friends before I went to Stratford Military School and continued our friendship over the year while attending Stratford! Two things I kept mindful of; first, be respectful to all where it applies, yes or no sir or mama, second carry my bookbag with my class materials in it "always be prepared". I was sometimes teased because of this way of conducting myself at school. It was o.k. with me, because I was focused!

My dad, an Atlantic City Police Officer, was working extra duty, in uniform at the Shore Park High Raise, located 225 North Virginia Avenue. Dad was in the lobby approximately 7:30 pm, when a couple exited the elevator, spoke to him, and proceeded out the rear exist. Moments later, my dad heard a loud shotgun blast. The female came running, screaming in shock back into the ground floor lobby! My dad responded, only yards away, where he found the male companion lying in a pool of blood, shot to death. The female companion had blood on her, but wasn't physically wounded. My dad was also unharmed responding so quickly!

My high school years at A.C.H.S. will always be remembered. Several guys and I started a high school social club, we were known as the Condors. We met every other week on Friday nights. Some of the things we did for recognition at Atlantic City High included holding dances, bus trips to school championship basketball games and bowling parties. That summer after we had started the Condors, my parents rented our bottom apartment to three young southern college men. They came up for the summer to work, holding down two jobs, saving some money to return to college by mid-August. They worked at the old Howard Johnson located at Arkansas and Pacific Avenues, now known as Caesar's Hotel Casino and the Club Harlem, located on the unit block, North Kentucky Avenue, Thursday night thru Sunday morning breakfast show. They were members of

Omega Psi Phi Fraternity, Inc. The Club Harlem had a strong connection with the Ques! Many of their Fraternity Brothers would stop by and visit them. I can remember one of the Omega men that lived downstairs; his handle name was Co-Co. The Fraternity Brothers had total respect, support, and brotherhood. Being the only male child in my family, becoming an Omega man started being a dream, and one day turned into reality. (More details will be forthcoming)!

The Upsilon Alpha Graduate Chapter of Omega Psi Phi Fraternity, Inc., agreed to sponsor our social club the Condors, as their little brothers. We changed our name to Omicron Nu Epsilon, Fraternity. Our colors were purple and gold. The motto was, "all for O.N.E. and O.N.E for all!" Our advisors from Upsilon Alpha graduate chapter of Omega Psi Phi, Inc. were Mr. Buddy Ward and Mr. Norman Williams, both have since entered into Omega Chapter!

Those who wanted to join had to be voted in, in order to pledge. Then, they had to complete a pledge period. Some members who continued on to higher education in college, one day would pledge Omega Psi Phi Fraternity, Inc., where "Friendship is essential to the Soul".

In June, 1974 the end of my junior year (11th grade) I, along with seven other juniors, was chosen to serve on our yearbook staff. We had two faculty teachers to help direct us with our project. We were the class of 1975! I took on the role of lay-out editor, designing the pattern of photos on each page. Because of our time element, meeting deadlines for photographs of groups such as track and field, social clubs, and rowing teams near the foot of the Albany Avenue Bridge, I strongly had begun to understand what a team player was all about. It involved helping or filling in for one another for a common goal, the goal to publish an outstanding yearbook for our Class of 1975!

Around the same time of year, when I was chosen for the yearbook staff, I joined the Atlantic City Volunteer Fire Reserve. I was the youngest male from a group of about twenty people including some women. I was the only high school student. I was an active member in the reserve. We normally responded to second alarm fires. Our job at the fire scene was adding additional lines (holes) and setting up additional lighting assisting A.C.F.D. During that time, you could be called anytime of the day, night, weekdays, weekends or weather conditions.

My first class of the day during my senior year was gym. Sometimes just hours earlier, I was at a second alarm fire; therefore, if I weren't ready for gym, it was no big deal. I was excused from taking gym that morning. My gym teacher realized that I was a volunteer firefighter. There were a number of second alarm fires during the time I served. Since I had been a volunteer with the City for about 16 months, in the summer of 1976, I, along with about eight other college students, was hired as a Special Police Officer. " And the beat goes on!"

Chapter Two

"Moving Right Along"

This was the nation's bicentennial year, July 4th, our country's two hundredth Birthday! Our uniform's colors were red, white and blue. Our main purpose was to perform public relations information to tourist on any given questions they may ask; direct bicyclists off the Boardwalk when riding their bike after hours; reporting lost children and reuniting found youngsters to whom they belonged. Although we didn't carry guns, we had the power to arrest. That summer, special events in 1976, we (special seasonal police) along with teams of law-enforcement provided security for the Freedom Train in celebration of the America Bicentennial. This train stopped at numerous cities across the nation with documents on display of the constitution, bill of rights and the first flag made by Ms. Betsy Ross with thirteen stars and stripes. Our country's history was well on its way to being the greatest!

The Miss America Parade was normally held about two weeks after Labor Day. Most seasonal special police officers had returned to college if not before, definitely on Labor Day. Furthering my education at the nearby Atlantic Community College, I was fortunate to work up to the Miss America Parade.

I enjoy helping and meeting people. I have met so many people from all over the state, country and world on the Boardwalk in Atlantic City. I met and had a nice conversation with the late Mayor Maynard Jackson of Atlanta, Georgia. He was leaning against the railing looking at the activity on the Boardwalk, standing at Park Place and the Boardwalk. Mayor Jackson also was taking in some cool ocean breeze and sunshine. I was a seasonal special police officer for the City of Atlantic City, summer of 1976, 1977, and 1978 while being a full-time criminal justice student at Atlantic Community College. At this time, I would like to share this with my readers. The thirteen hundred block of Atlantic Avenue, which sits between South Carolina and Tennessee Avenues from the Boardwalk to Route Thirty was my work zone. My employment locations were A & P Supermarket, Dandy's Men's Clothing, A.C. Townhouses, Shore Park, V.A. and Mediterranean Avenue (security while most were under construction), Woolworth's 5 & 10 located on the 1300 Boardwalk and City Hall, the Police Department, and City Welfare. On July 16, 1979 about twenty people including myself were sworn in as Atlantic City Police Officers. The group sworn in consisted of employees that worked in different divisions of public safety, such as Communication Bureau, Special Police Officers, or City Clerk positions. It consisted of about seven women and thirteen men.

We attended a mini Police Academy that was approximately three weeks long before hitting the street for sworn duty. We had training in criminal law - searching suspects, giving them their rights, physical fitness and firearms safety, cleaning and safekeeping our weapons, and shoot to kill only if the suspect is armed with a gun or knife threatening bodily harm to the general public, co-workers or self. The Academy was located in Atlantic City near Martin Luther King Boulevard on Route 30 west bound - "Old school". Today, the tunnel, (roadway) which you can take to Brigantine or the other three (3) casino locations has taken its place where the Police Academy and Pistol Range once stood! This roadway connects you from the Marina Area, Route 30, mid-town, The Walk and Atlantic City Expressway. Upon completion of the mini Academy, there were two shifts available to work, first, 8 a.m. until 4 p.m.; second, 4 p.m. until 12 midnight. You worked with a veteran officer under the Safe Street unit, foot patrol in a district, getting to know the people who lived and worked in your district of patrol - patrol on routine, yet not becoming routine. Some mini academy officers may have been placed in a patrol car riding with a veteran officer as a team unit, learning the ropes as it was said among the veteran officers.

The Boardwalk was my usual patrol area on foot. Although at times, I was paired off with a veteran officer on foot in the south side inlet of the city. These areas included Main to New Jersey Avenue, and Atlantic Avenue to the Boardwalk. The area that I patroled was a heavily populated Spanish community, mostly good residents, taking care of their families in some difficult times. There were a lot of arson fires, some open market drug activities and those having warrants for their arrest from the county or out of state, living with their family in the South Inlet. I was one officer that was trusted, respected and loved. On Sunday, I never had to worry about getting something to eat or watching an N.F.L. game on T.V; a door was always open for my partner and me to stop in and escape the outdoor elements - rain, cold and heat.

In Mid-April of 1980, my group that was sworn in July of 1979, along with some additional new recruits and three officers from another Atlantic County jurisdiction (township/city) completed our state certification of basic police training that consisted of the basic fourteen weeks. It was truly made up of blood, sweat and tears. The price I paid to become one of Atlantic City's Finest! It was only through the will of Jesus and having His grace that I graduated! During that fourteen- week basic training course, we may have had about nine women at this time in the Police Academy. At that time, this was the most women to enter the Atlantic City Police Academy at any given time.

Mrs. Maggie Creswell, first woman hired as a police officer in the state of New Jersey, performed her duties very well - outstanding job with the teenage girls in the city. Mrs. Creswell meant business; if you were told by her to get in order with your conduct, especially violating the city curfew for juveniles, you listened! May Jesus continue to bless her spirit. As a child, I was aware of Mrs. Creswell because she belonged to a group of police officers' wives who had a social club that met bi-weekly. They performed community service throughout the city.

Having females in class, was kind of difficult for them to climb over a six foot wall, clearing the other side with dog dropping in which one can fall or land in. Some older male recruits could have the same problem. Two other recruits from another police department were joined up by a third officer. This officer had transferred from an out-of-state police agency, and would only attend when we covered 2c law. While on a fifteen minute break, the handler would go to his police vehicle, let the K-9 out to relieve itself in the area of the wall. Some took it as a joke, especially the two officers to whom the department the dog belonged.

A couple of days later, I was duty officer. All recruits got a chance at this. It was for the entire day in training, "Officer of the Day". It was designed to place you in a leadership position, which allowed you to be responsible for helping conduct others in the Academy with taking roll call, supervising, cleaning up the areas, (classroom/break room or outside) trash, common or simple orders. Near the end of the day, when it was time to clean up for the next group of police cadets that were starting at 5 p.m., I ordered the two others in the departmental K-9 to "clean up its dropping" by the wall. One of the guys flatly refused, I reported him to the staff; it was taken care of by his other department colleague. The K-9 handler would leave after the 2C law discussion was over. I didn't want to see people having additional fear after climbing the wall and landing in it (K-9 droppings).

Several days later, the guy who refused to clean up after his department's K-9, had his turn to be officer of the day. Around 3 p.m. that day before the physical fitness work out for our class, I started getting a headache. I didn't say anything to anyone and attempted to participate. We went on a three-mile run. It was hot that day and the sun was very bright. Just a couple of hundred feet from the Academy, the class had stopped jogging and was jogging in place. I was trailing in the rear of the pack of recruits when all of a sudden, a hand out of nowhere, hit me in the chest. I felt the pain go from my head to my chest which was the point of impact. I was looking downward at the ground at the time of impact. I saw a glare on the ground, it was an empty 16 oz. soda glass bottle; turning my head upward, and all I could see was this guy laughing because of his actions. I picked up the bottle off the ground and tried to take his head off, but was stopped by others that were nearby. We both were called in the staff office immediately. Because of my headache, I was not thinking. I should have placed him under arrest for assault. I told one of the instructors that was present in the office and he asked me why my eyes were glazed and red. I told them to send me to the hospital for drug testing, and then be prepared for a lawsuit. Then, I won't have to be a police officer and can retire from the suit won. I truly believe I surprised the academy staff supervisors in suggesting that I go to the hospital because of the severe headache that was out of control, due to the fact that the officer of the day hit me in the chest for no apparent, justified reason. They decided not to send me to the hospital; the incident was dropped but not the pain from my headache.

The Academy instructors seemed to have had their own agenda, washing out certain police recruits. There were a couple of incidents that stood out in my mind. First, another police recruit who had transferred from an inner city police department, Trenton, New Jersey; he was certified by the state in police training. He had to go through and complete a full fourteen (14) weeks basic course for Police Training. Now, the officer that transferred into this state only came to the Police Academy for State Law, 2c who also allowed his K-9 loose. The K-9 would go near the wall to relieve itself. This made it more difficult for those who had to struggle to the top of the wall and then have enough energy to push them off of it to clear the K-9 dropping.

Lastly, there was a married couple in our session known as the thirty-third sessions. They were doing just fine with their class assignments, physical training, exam results and having the right attitude as officers of law-enforcement.

When our class finally reached the last stage of training, weapon safety and target practice on the range, the husband could not get the required score of seventy (70) to pass. We were there for a week, Monday thru Friday. On one cold rainy night, the husband was not able to score over seventy, and had a few recruits worried about his eligibility. On the last day at the range, just hours left in our workday, the Deputy Commissioner of Public Safety appeared unexpectedly. He took the husband's weapon out of his holster, and walked up to the range towel, asking the assistant range master to adjust the weapon sight. The weapon was returned to the husband's holster. He went on the line to try again to qualify as instructed by the Deputy Commissioner of Public Safety. This time he passed! His score was about eighty-nine points (89). This move stopped him from being terminated from the thirty-third session of the Atlantic City Police Academy.

The range master supervisor who claims to know about firearms was shortly transferred to the patrol division, four to twelve shifts. This supervisor was involved in a shooting that left a young woman paralyzed. The supervisor spotted a fleeing suspect wanted in connection of a theft out of the Sands Casino. He opened fire on the suspect near Mt. Vernon and Pacific Avenues, in which two rookie foot patrol officers saw the supervisor discharge his weapon and they did the same. Because of the accidental shooting of the female victim, a settlement was reached. If they could have gotten the bullet from her, it would have been determined whose weapon it came from. What is certain is that the bullet came from an officer's weapon! Soon after, the supervisor retired!

After graduation July 11th, 1980 the 33rd session was ready for the streets. They placed most of the recruits into the patrol, or foot patrol. "Safe Street" was the name of our game. The two shifts were, 8 a.m., until 4 p.m. or 4 p.m. until midnight. I got lucky, I was walking a beat and had a female partner that joined the police department the same time I did. We have worked many times together. I sometimes worked alone or had a female partner. It did not matter to me, because we had each other's back, and was going home safe at the end of the shift. Other than the Boardwalk, my beat was mainly, Martin L. King to South Carolina, and Arctic to Adriatic Avenues. I had graduated from Atlantic Community College about two years before the academy, but I pushed forward to attend Stockton State College, a four-year college.

Chapter Three

"To Protect and Serve"

At this time I was working about four hours a night from 8 p.m. until 12 midnight at the Lincoln Motel at the corner of North Carolina and Adriatic Avenues. I basically kept the juveniles and some disorderly persons in check. I had a good relationship with the staff (front office/ motel manager). I only worked three nights a week. One night, the desk clerk, Ozzie, asked me to give him a ride to his second job at the Resorts Casino, located up the street. I hung up the phone telling him I was on my way from my house. Just as I arrived, I pulled up in my Volvo at the motel office and was exiting my vehicle when a male came running out of the motel's driveway located in the rear. About eight seconds later, the manager, Sal came out yelling "Wesley! Wesley!" I got back into my vehicle. The male ran across the street, running at break-neck speed! His hands were not on the side swinging. His hands were in a position as though he had something in his hands. I pulled off, telling Sal to call the police and have them come into the area, I needed backup!

The male ran onto a vacant lot at the corner of North Carolina and Drexel Avenues. I never took my eyes off the suspect whom I was chasing in my car. The male had disrobed, leaving his ski mask on, which had a round ball on top. He ducked behind some cars that were parked there. I knew where he was because of the hat that he was wearing. I got out of my vehicle, turned on the high beam lights, and then walked up to him, grabbing him with my left hand, while holding the weapon with my right hand. He was placed face down in a puddle of water. I knew he had a gun by the speed that he was running and not seeing his hands swinging on the side of his body. I knelt on his back ordering him not to move; he brought his head up, I put my weapons barrel to the back of his head and cocked the hammer back, telling him that I was the police. "Put it down in the puddle now", I yelled and he complied. The motel manager informed the backup officers of my location, which consisted of Patrol, Vice, K-9, and supervisors, those who were available that responded. I was off in the distance from the Lincoln Motel, which is where the male suspect was searched, cuffed and taken into City Hall. Several officers and I searched the entire lot, under cars in the area in which he tried to hide. No weapons were found at that time of arrest. I was never given the chance to take Ozzie, the evening clerk, to his second job at the Resorts Casino.

I went into City Hall for reports to be made about the incident. The suspect was sitting in the Vice Squad Office still in handcuffs.

One of the Vice Officers came in with a broken gold chain; the suspect stated that the gold chain belonged to him.

The Vice Officer stated, "Then these are your drugs because the chain was lying on the coat, and the drugs were inside the coat pocket". It was later established that the suspect went inside a motel room and stuck-up its occupants for drugs and money. Just as I pulled up to pick-up Ozzie, he ran out of the room, passing the motel manager who alerted me.

That morning about five hours later, during Roll Call, I informed the officer that had the beat next to mine that covered the area of my midnight apprehension. The Sun was brightly shining and it was still cold at about 8:15 a.m. The officer later recovered a sawed off shotgun. It was located near the site of the arrest of the suspect. No children had noticed it on their way to school, and neither did anybody else. A weapon was off the street, helping with the safety of the public. Give Jesus, the praise in all He does!

From the previous incident that occurred at the Lincoln Motel, I was on my day off from duty, Safe Streets Patrol 8 a.m. to 4 p.m. I worked extra duty through the casino detail unit. With this unit you can work on your day off or hours before, or after you put in eight hours of normal duty for the city.

You would call to schedule the extra duty detail, about a week before it happens. Once accepting the extra assignment, it was your responsibility to cover that detail. The casino that you worked for would pay the city for your hours worked; you would get paid for those hours, on the off week of City pay day. I, along with three other officers, was working for the Castle Casino, also known as Trump Marina, near the Back Maryland (as known by its residents). The street leading into the casino property, had just been paved and it had to be striped (Traffic Lanes). It was about 6 p.m. and it was dark and the traffic signals were temporarily off; therefore, we were doing some kind of traffic duty. I was lighting the flares about three lanes, with about fifteen flares in each lane. This was done for an hour and half; my vision from lighting all those flares had an effect on my eyes. I got off at 7:30 p.m. that night after doing my eight hours of extra duty. I went directly home, only to meet my dad who asked if I would fill in for him at the Lincoln Motel that evening. It was just for four hours – 8 p.m. until midnight; so I agreed. Ozzie, the night clerk, gave me a room to relax in because I normally stand on the corner to make my presence known to the police in the area - chilling out, it's Wild, Wild, Wes on duty, I was looking at the television in a room that faced Adriatic Avenue, and across the street was the driveway, parking lot for the Six Bedrooms, the Public Housing Complex. When I heard a knock on the door, it was a friend of mine who lived down the street. He saw my car parked outside and came down to talk. I lay across the bed closing my eyes, trying to get focused away from the flares that I lit during the casino detail, and all of a sudden my friend called me to the door which was cracked open. Across the street there were two males, one on the driver side of a taxicab and the other was standing in the rear right side of the cab. The male near the driver had what appeared to be a shotgun on him. It was a stick-up in progress! I didn't have an assigned Tac-radio at this time. I called the motel office, and was patched through to police communications. I informed them who I was, where I was, and what was occurring. I told them to have units come in with their sirens and flashing police lights, off Route Thirty (30) and North Carolina Avenue into the public housing projects (Six Bedrooms). I had the males in sight as I ran across the street ducking behind some bushes and parked cars. I had a clear shot at them, but the flare was still affecting my vision. Although brick structures were in the background of these armed males, I chose not to discharge my weapon at them, because I didn't want any innocent person to get hurt. The cab driver backed up moving to the street he had stopped, and I shouted out to him "Police! Are you okay? I have my back-up on the way." Just at that second they arrived blocking off the area, the males had gotten away. They ran into one of the housing units in the six-bedroom section, no one was hurt and they took about forty dollars from the driver. Because of that incident, I asked my safe street supervisor if I could take a Tac radio with me for my extra duty details, allowing me to have communications with the command center. My request was granted! One night, I was working Resorts Casino from 1 a.m. until 9 a.m., where I had just finished a four-to-twelve shift in safe streets. After I got a fully charged battery for my Tac radio about 12:45, I was driving into Resorts Casino in the unit block of South Virginia Avenue when I smelled smoke. I got out of my car and saw smoke pouring from a two story building. Using my Tac radio I called in the location of the fire, requesting them to send the Fire Department. The dwelling appeared to be occupied; I ran up the front steps to the porch and knocked on the door screaming "Get out! Help is on the way". I kicked in the door, but I was unable to get to the person who had a leg cast on that was bedridden, on the next level up. I ran back outside and tried to climb up to the porch's roof; I was unable to reach him. He was standing in the window and I told him to jump or fall out. At that moment, the fire department arrived and was able to reach the victim, who experienced little harm. I was so blessed to have a radio. Within a week, Safe Streets started allowing us, to take our radios home. Eventually, we were assigned radio charges to keep at home; therefore, having communications was another tool in fighting the war on crime and providing safety for the public. During this time I enrolled in classes at Stockton State College in Pomona. I was a full-time student, paying for classes out of my pocket - a very good investment that has stood the hands of time, while I was at Stockton State College.

I met a good friend. We both pledged Omega Psi Phi. I had to drop line because of my responsibility with the Police Department. I pledged underground for about a month, officially resigning from pledging after a Roy Ayers concert held in the gym at Stockton State College. But I continued to support my then line brothers in bringing in bake goods for sales, and helping transport Brothers up to Glassboro State College (Rowan University) for sessions with their pledging line of Omega. I gave one guy, who was my friend that crossed into Omega an application for the Atlantic City Police Department. He took the Civil-Service Police Exam and went to the front of the list being a veteran and became a sworn police officer in 1980, the 34th session. He graduated from the Atlantic City Police Academy the class after mine; the thirty-fourth session was his graduation class. He also pledged Omega Psi Phi Fraternity at Stockton State College. Robert Medley was my fellow co-worker and just down the road my Fraternity Brother of Omega Psi Phi Fraternity, Inc.

I was working Alpha platoon safe streets units, day time shift 8 p.m. to 4 p.m.; my dad was on the same Shift mobile patrol, in a car with a partner - both had seniority with weekends off. Anyway, I came into City Hall to stand roll call at the sergeant's desk about 7:44 a.m.; moments later an unnamed officer came in still putting his utility belt on. After roll call, I went to the safe streets office to find out what was my assignment that day, and I was told by the captain I was late and I explained to him I stood roll call. Also I was there before they said fall in for roll-call. He stated I was late because I should have reported in first. Nothing was ever said about the other officer who walked in during roll call. I insisted I wasn't late, but the Captain got bent out of shape almost said the N-word, but caught himself. The next thing I knew I was transferred to Charlie platoon midnight to 8 a.m. in patrol in a police vehicle. I could not believe that this happened in March, the few classes that I had taken at Stockton State College were not in jeopardy because of my new hours of work, so I continued to press on for my degree in criminal justice!

Chapter Four

"Charlie - The Real Deal"

M y first night on Charlie platoon, the officer that I was assigned to was Henry Charles a veteran of the force for about five years. He would show me the ropes on how to work as a team player on Charlie Platoon; we would back-up/or ride into the area of trouble, incase units were needed. We worked very hard on Charlie; during the weeknights, it seemed after 4 a.m. when the casino floor closed, it would get quiet, but prior to closing it would be business as usual.

That particular shift when we were not busy, we parked our vehicle out on the ground of the Police Academy. There were a few back ends of a tractor-trailer, so we went between them not being able to be seen by the public or mainly our supervisors. One time the patrol car was running, the lights were off and we had unsnapped our ties and closed our eyes. We could hear the radio transmission if any, sometimes if they called a particular unit and they didn't get a response, in about thirty seconds later a high-pitched squeal would sound that would mean listen to radio. Normally, it was an attention signal; anyway, we were relaxing when I heard Henry say "O.k. en route." I opened my eyes, looking over at him, he put the dome light on the inside the car and said White Tower, Missouri_and Atlantic there is a disorderly person. I started writing it down on our activity log sheet. I snapped my tie on and we rolled out to the call. When we pulled up to the location - White Tower, Missouri_and Atlantic Avenues, Henry said over the car radio "Alpha four, fifty-three" (out of service) moments later the dispatcher said "For what?" Henry responded, "Motor vehicle stop." and read the license tags of an unoccupied vehicle parked outside of White Tower. Moments later he said "Professional courtesy given S.O.W." (sent on way).

Brother Charles is a member of Omega Psi Phi Fraternity, Inc. Eventually I started working with a rookie officer freshly out of high school and former beach patrol, "lifeguard"! Because I was senior in the car and my partner wanted to learn how to serve the public and protect it, he always looked forward to driving the entire shift; I had one rule, do not move this car without my having full knowledge where we may be sent. No matter how minor it may seem! I don't want to wake up to gunshots or where I would not have knowledge of the circumstances. My partner was a good person, all that piss and vinegar that he displayed took a back seat in learning his sworn duties. After working a few months together as a team, I will now explain the following:

41

My partner had court one morning in Superior Court in Mays Landing, New Jersey, approximately 25 miles west of Atlantic City; he reported to the police garage to get a car to drive to Mays Landing by 9 a.m. When my partner got to the police garage, another officer who was not on the up and up, I would say, a problem child also needed a ride to Mays landing for another case which also started at 9 a.m. Someone who was working at the garage gave this problem child cop a new police car that was scheduled to be painted and have police decoys, transforming it into a marked unit to be used in patrol. This person owed the P.C. Officer; so, he got to use the vehicle, and my partner was a passenger going to Mays landing. The driver of the new police vehicle put a crease on the front right side by hitting a guard rail going over the Delilah Road overpass going to Mays Landing. It was discovered when it went for a makeover (mark patrol unit), my partner stated he dropped P.C. Officer off on Route Thirty near his home in back of W.U.S.S in Venice Park (AM Radio Station). My partner then drove directly to the police garage, dropped off the city car, and drove his personal vehicle home. The next day Pete was informed to see the Captain, who was in charge of the police garage, the problem child officer never signed the vehicle out. The damage to the new vehicle was discovered just before its decaled as a marked unit for patrol. The Captain wanted to know three things - What happened? Where did it happen? Who was responsible for it? The Captain gave Pete two options. (1) Tell, in order to keep your employment with the force, or (2) Don't tell, and you will lose your job because you are still on probation. My partner loved his job and wanted it; so, he told what had happened and who was responsible. Because of my partner's cooperation, some unknown officers would cut him off from his transmission when he would transmit on the radio. Most of the time I would do the talking on radio and kept the paper work in order, that was handed in at the end of shift. Another morning at the end of the shift, I dropped Pete off at the rear of City Hall to take our equipment in (log sheet & paperwork and shotgun). My partner put his personal things in the trunk of his car, then he opened the driver side door, and he jumped out screaming as I was pulling off. I hit my brakes then jumped out my car, thinking I ran over his foot or something, he pointed at his driver's side. I walked over and looked inside his car someone had used a Jimmy (device to open cars) shot a ten inch rat and placed it on a newspaper in the driver's seat. My partner had sat on it, realizing it the human side of him, he began to scream! We both also realized that being a working team, we had to step our game up, because among us there were some immature officers. Individuals that we had to put up with, we started to see by their actions on calls who had our back and who didn't. Working together, being steady partners, sharing a car to patrol, likes, dislikes, and further goals, are some of the many things we discussed during the time to "Protect and Serve". My partner had a detail at new casino that was to open to the public. The detail was from 9 a.m. until 5 p.m. He had just gotten off his regular tour of duty at the casino when he was placed in a room with money that was wrapped in bricks placed on palettes - hundreds, fifties, twenties, fives and one dollar bills; his job was to watch them dispense the money to where it had to go in the casino hotel. He was sitting in a chair and started dozing off. There were no windows nor fresh air, with all that money. You could only imagine what if. . . cameras filming your every move or no move. Someone called into the police department and reported he was sleeping. It was caught on tape, whoever responded or should have seen the tape suggested a thirty day suspension without pay. Being suspended for thirty days without pay was kind of heavy- handed. It made me start to think what was the purpose? Pete went up to New York City and worked as a Laborer for one of his brother's pipe fitting unions. Because he was suspended, the shift supervisors assigned me as turnkey. My responsibility was to assist the Desk Sergeant in taking personal property - money, belts, shoe strings, and anything that could pose a threat to fellow inmates, themselves, or officers working as turn-keys. I would normally let persons who get processed get one phone call, do a walk by their cell about six times an hour to check on them from hurting themselves or not needing any medical attention. All because of my shift, I would have a radio or my personal tape player and began to listen to music of popular singing groups. One inmate yelled out to another and said "Officer Hawkins' music that he plays make me realize that I'm not coming in here anymore, I miss my freedom and I would never see her again". I would get to work about eleven thirty and get off some time by seven o'clock.

Officer Vahuff, an officer that had a lot of seniority of the shift and was well liked and respected by all. Believe me, there was never a dull moment as turnkey. I used that position to my advantage, by studying, reading, & writing reports on team papers. It grew on me, I really liked it. One night I was sitting in my work cubical, doing some paperwork when I heard a loud knock at the door which was locked. I got up from my desk, proceeded to open the door. It was my partner Pete, "Hey man!" he said, we were glad to see and greet each other. He told me he was back; he had picked up some work out of state during his suspension working with one of his brothers. Pete wanted to know if we could team-up again as partners. I said "Yes, no problem!" He was due back to work in a couple of days and requested to make out professional mark on Charlie Platoon!

Chapter Five

"Bringing Me Closer"

M y partner's first night back from his thirty day suspension was a very foggy night. There was a report of a fatal accident at Ohio and Route 30. We heard many different units give out of service transmissions (53) at that location. He drove directly from the police garage that was located off of Huron Avenue - a half mile from the scene of the fatal accident. It was not in our district, but we had to fill up the gas tank. Therefore, we had a little time to spare before putting our unit in service in our assigned district. I sat in the car filling out our log sheets while he and the many Police and Fire personnel walked about thirty yards to see what was going on. He came back to the car and said, "Yo man, I want to show you something". I reluctantly went with him to see this accident scene. It was a med-sized convertible that was heading East on Route 30. The Tractor- trailer had pulled out of Ohio Ave onto Route 30, and stopped to make a left turn, making it go Westbound on Route 30, going out of the City. It had blocked the East Bound Lanes. It was foggy and the trailer didn't appear to have any reflecting material to be visible in such foggy conditions. It appeared to me the driver never saw the tractor trailer and drove under it causing the drivers head to become unattached from his torso; his head was lying in the back seat of the car, and one hand was on the steering wheel, the other was on the radio knob that turns the station or adjust the volume. I believe the convertible had its top down because it was visible (body & head) and with my flash light, in plain view from where we stood next to the convertible car. Also there were no skid marks. The State, very shortly after this fatal accident, put in a barricade that prevented a car or vehicle to exit from Ohio Avenue to head westbound out of town. Our last call on that shift was to see the manager at a restaurant about a break-in that occurred over night. It was only ten minutes remaining before our new shift would relieve us from duty, we took the call without any reservation. This restaurant was a place where my girlfriend and I ate on Wednesday night, each week because of their baby back ribs special, including all the ribs you could eat. The female manager met us at the front door of the restaurant. We could see the cash register was smashed open and the radio was snatched out, leaving wires exposed in the front cabinet, used for restaurant business. We then walked to the rear in the kitchen area; it was dark, and my partner and the woman stopped at the cage. It was from the floor to the ceiling with a chain and a pad lock used to secure it. This is where they kept the liquor for the business. The lock and chain were snatched out from the cage. My partner and the manager went further back to turn on the lights. Meanwhile, I am walking, checking out other areas in the kitchen. I was standing next to the dishwasher when the lights came on, I looked up and drew my weapon, "Damn" I remember saying, there was a wall of roaches that formed an image of a person standing up. I began to think it was going to attack me, because of its image that formed, and then the manager walked over to my location in the kitchen. She seemed to be embarrassed of the infestation, immediately, and asked if she could give us some comps for us to use at a later date to come in and eat. We both refused. Upstairs over the restaurant were apartments. From that point, I don't eat at restaurants with people living above it. I wrote the report up and notified the Health Department of that situation. I'm very choosey where I dine and they bring my food from the back (kitchen) didn't hold water with me!

Our next tour of working together was October 14th, 1981 (M.L.K won the Nobel Prize1964) It was another wet, foggy cold night with very little going on, sometimes it was known as "Quiet before the storm". Police being requested, was for mostly alarms that were unfounded of a break-in, motor vehicle stops issuing warnings, to parties and sending them on their way. About 2:20 a.m. several units met over at Moe's Chicken located at this time in the nine hundred Block Absecon Boulevard. We ordered some gizzards, wings, fries and soft drinks. We got our orders and met up again at the High Gate Apartments building located on the six hundred block of Absecon Boulevard. The High Gate was under construction at the time; we parked in the rear of the site, had conversations and ate chicken. A couple other units joined us, it was about seven units holding shop! My partner and I were talking about the call to the restaurant the prior morning. A loud, squealing sound came across that radio and it got our attention. A patrol unit was stopped by a young hooker named "Sunshine" (street name). She was only nineteen and spotted the male, she had signed a John Doe warrant for assault. She spotted the male driving a brown Chrysler Markee down near the Golden Nugget. A few blocks away she stopped a patrol unit informing them what had happened. At that very moment the suspect had pulled on the left side of the police car, waiting on the traffic light. They were east bound from the Golden Nugget Casino, on Pacific Avenue. Sunshine screamed, "Stop that motherfucker". The suspect ran the light to get away, but a few blocks away, he had pulled over. A second police unit, backup, arrived at the motor vehicle stop. The suspect then again jetted off starting a high speed pursuit. This was the second time with him pulling off and the sound of the high frequency made everyone listen to their radio. All the units that were at the High Gate started to pull out to get to the aid of our co-workers. My partner and I drove to Arkansas and Baltic, the entrance to the Atlantic City Expressway. Our police lights were on; once we reached the location, the suspect changed his path of direction away from the Expressway Entrance. Therefore, we drove down Arkansas Avenue against traffic with lights and sirens on. I saw several units at high speed, drive down Atlantic Avenue.

We made it to Atlantic Avenue and turned right off of Arkansas to Atlantic; at that point, I started loading the shot-gun, and jack one, into the chamber, ready to be used if needed. The pursuit was two blocks from Atlantic Avenue, horizontal from where we were. We got over to Arctic Avenue and Dover, turning to our left, heading westbound on Arctic / Winchester Avenue. We came along side of the Sunoco Gas Station at the foot of the Albany Avenue Bridge; the pursuit was about to pass in front of us, when my partner hit the gas and joined in. We turned in; we had the suspect sandwiched in as we approached the top of the bridge. I went to take the shotgun out of the holder, and my partner said, "Leave it in". I told him no, because if this car cut off and the way I was positioned in the car it would be easier to return fire with the shotgun. Just at that time he unsnapped his holster, the suspect's vehicle slowed up firing a shot to his left and then shot into our car striking my partner which I didn't realize until moments later. He yelled "Mom", turn the steering wheel to his left causing the suspect's car and our police vehicle to collide, making us spin out of control! Pete, fell onto me, I said "Pete, Pete shaking his shoulder! I got no response, my hands were saturated in blood, I looked over to my right. I could see the suspect image looking at me from his car, I opened the car door and my training kicked in, as a shotgun shell was already waiting in the chamber to take this suspect out!

No judge, nor jury, his time was to be served. I stepped out in front of other officers who drew their weapons at the suspect! A few co-workers said "When I jumped out the car holding the shotgun, I was in their line of fire, they pointed their weapons into the air". Giving me an advantage to strike the suspect, (target) and bring it to a close, in which I did! I laid the shotgun in the door well, grabbed the car mike and said "Clear the air, clear the air, officer down, my partner is down". Communications asked "What unit is this and what is your location?". I told them my unit number and I was on top of the Albany Avenue Bridge, and a bunch of cops ran over to my vehicle! They helped me pull him out the car, they placed Pete in a nearby police car and attempted to save his life. But one guy lost it just as they passed the monument at Ventnor and Albany Avenue. I was stripped of the shotgun and my weapon carry in my holster. I walked over to the suspect's car. He was lying on the ground in a pool of blood, with a massive hole in his forehead! He looked to have brain matter coming out of his wound. I tried to kick his head off; but was grabbed, and placed in a nearby patrol car to get me out of the area.

I was taken to City Hall and placed in the office of Special Investigation Unit. More officers that were involved started showing up and we retraced the whole situation. Using a black board and chalk to go step by step understanding what had happened. A phone call was made to my father, telling him to come into City Hall right away. It had to do with me! As he was getting dressed, my mother decided she was going also. They both were on their way within moments. My dad told me, they were at Delaware and Baltic Avenue, when over the radio, a special bulletin was announced "Officer shot and killed, more details soon to come". My mom said she just lost it, my father ran every light using caution to get to City Hall, to find out what was going on! My mother saw me, and hugged me, crying out of control! I told her I was alright, and wanted to get to the hospital to see my partner, Pete! I was then, at that time, informed that he had passed, I lost it! I started getting out of control, emotionally and physically. It was suggested that I be taken to the hospital to be checked out. My parents drove me there; inside were co-workers that had been caught up in the bridge incident or parts of the pursuit. They were in shock, waiting on the doctor to be discharged, when they saw me and it all started over again - everyone got emotional! The hospital staff pushed me into an Emergency Room to get me away, from my co-workers. The area they put me in had a male on a table with his head bandage with a pump and holes in his mouth, helping him to stay alive. It was the suspect holding on to life but yet he took my partner's life! I went for my gun, realizing I didn't have it. I then tried to snatch some surgery knives, trying to do more harm to him. The hospital nurses, doctors and some security people came running into the treatment room that I was in. They began to apologize for putting me in the same room as the suspect, who was later identified! The doctor tried to give me some kind of needle to calm me down; I refused and walked out the hospital! My dad drove me over to my partner's home in Venice Park. I spoke with his mother and said, "He loved you, he called your name. . .Mom"! We hugged each other and I left. I got home about 6:15 a.m. and went upstairs to my parents, I went under the kitchen sink and got scotch belonging to my parents poured a stiff drink, and chased it down with milk. About twenty minutes later, unexpectedly, Henry Charles also a member of Omega Psi Phi came to my house. He took me over to his home. There were other co-workers involved there. We were hidden, out in Venice Park, food and liquor, subs from White House Subs were served. I passed out, most of the guys had left when I woke up about 5 p.m. Henry later took me to Bible Study at Second Baptist Church on Center Street. I have some history with this church from a very young age as a child going to church with my mother and sister, serving on the Junior Usher Board as a youth. The Reverend I. S. Cole was our Shepherd, that evening. I totally lost it, again. I cried like a baby - the sadness of my partner's death, how my life was sparred and thinking I would not gain eternity in going to Heaven to meet internally my Holy Father. The reason was what I had done with the shotgun to the suspect. It was explained to me that Jesus controls everything through His Father, God the Almighty, and to hold on, He will see you through, I was told! Death was knocking at my door, three times in a twenty second period, on the bridge, that early morning!

My partner had on his bulletproof vest; I didn't have one. The scenario - (1) I was sitting next to my partner; the shots could have passed through him and got me also. (2) My partner was driving; we could had plunged off the side of the bridge, or (3), when I "Stepped out" with the shotgun to return fire, I could have gotten shot by officers that were behind our unit. Jesus' presence was in the car and on the bridge; even today I feel his presence on the bridge! Jesus took my partner home. After the smoke had cleared, the arsenal of high powered weapons discovered in the trunk of the suspect's vehicle, not including the 357 magnum, a forty-five and 9mm handgun in the front with him, along with rounds (cases) of ammunition. All weapons were in mint condition, and destroyed because it took my partner's life (a police officer). It could have been real ugly if the suspect had made it to his trunk of his car!

The viewing for my partner was held the night before his funeral. It was at Gormley's Funeral Home on Atlantic Avenue, a couple of businesses from a Fire House, located at California and Atlantic Avenue. The Fire House, known to many as Station Four (4), was used as a gathering place for people going to view my partner. There were hundreds of people and law enforcement officers paying their respect; the fire house helped out stay out of the light, steady rain and help long lines to get into the funeral home. It helped people to meet up with people inside Station Four. I was lead from the Fire House after viewing Pete to Tony's Baltimore Grill on the opposite end of the street, within walking distance. Once in at Tony's, I was sat on a stool bar, and the drinks just kept coming. Sorrow and pain were at its greatest seeing my partner, as if he were asleep! "Absent from the body is present with the Lord."

The next morning was the funeral service Police Officers, from around the nation were in attendance. The service was held at St. Nicholas, a Catholic Church located at Tennessee and Pacific Avenue in Atlantic City. I rode in my Volvo driven by a girlfriend; we were about the third vehicle following Pete's family Limousines. In the front of the funeral progression were approximately sixty motorcycles escorting the progression. When we reached Pleasantville, (about seven miles from Atlantic City), at the corner of Delilah and Main Street, it was later stated that the last car was passing the church when we were in Pleasantville. I estimated about an eight mile long funeral progression. The progression was heading for the Holy Cross Cemetery in Mays Landing, New Jersey, where he was laid to rest!

I had taken about a two week period off from work. I kept up with class assignments not to fall behind in my studies. I then returned back to work, "Charlie Platoon". I was taken off of Street Patrol, and was assigned to the desk sergeant as the utility driver. The responsibilities were helping the desk sergeant, including the booking of arrested persons, taking the names of officers calling out of work sick, special assignments at the request of street patrol, such as bringing barricades to cut off traffic or pavement, due to incidents or guard arrested persons /prisoners while at the hospital. Sometimes the utility driver would relieve a patrol unit from a location so it could get back into service.

One morning, I took some shotguns and additional ammunition/ shotguns out to Venice Park, on East Riverside Drive, regarding a barricade suspect with hostages. The Swat Team was alerted to respond, the materials were for the members of Swat!

It had ended peacefully with the suspect releasing the hostages and then surrendering to police. I also would pick-up orders of food for the desk sergeant, juvenile, and detective bureau if needed considering being a team player helping out where I could or requested for help, was not a problem with me.

I started taking more independent classes that met once a week, which dealt with research for the development of a term paper with professors and other classmates writing term papers due near the end of the semester.

Chapter Six

"Charlie, In The Dark, But Jesus Light Will Prevail!!!"

My focus was to graduate from Stockton, get off that shift (Charlie), and out of patrol. Having earned my bachelor of arts degree in Criminal Justice, doing something with policy or community relations more or less out of the frontline patrol. Somehow they put me permanently as turnkey. Therefore, I was not allowed to work on the streets on regular bases.

The inside man, some of my co-workers called me, joking around. I had gotten studying and working on my term papers down to a science, the only time I was seen or heard from was when I was helping out with some person being booked for lock-up. Other than that, I was studying at my desk, back in the jail. I will never forget one morning, about 3am,, the Captain (shift commander) came back to where I was working in my corner, inside the jail. I had books, note cards, and papers scattered all about on my desk. I was listening to some recorded music that I made at home. It helped relax inmates and myself. The captain asked what was I doing and I told him studying for classes that I was taking at Stockton State College. "Classes?", replied the Captain. "You have a good job, with great pay," he said. I reminded him it was not secure enough for me, for what I had been through. 'Enough is a must!' I was referring to uniform operations in the department. Later on that morning a couple of inmates started talking about how the music that was being played was going to keep them on the straight and narrow, and make a promise this would be the last time they would be in jail, and start to love themselves by having their freedom not because of a relationship with the opposite sex.

About three weeks later, I was in the jail because I had processed someone who had to be taken in the back for lockup. Roll call was being conducted. It was ordered by the shift commander, a different Captain to stay out of the unit South Indiana Avenue. A three-man stakeout team was on surveillance, because of the amounts of break-ins, on cars in that area. Later that mid-morning, I was asked by a detective bureau clerk to see if I could ride with him to pick-up some food from the Silver Dollar Saloon. They had great sandwiches and I got permission from the desk sergeant Murray Sr. who also requested to ordered some additional food for our team. I had on my black coat and my Stevie Wonder Hat (baseball style.) Tom drove his car to pick up the food. I was the passenger and we parked behind a medium sized car on Indiana Avenue, right around the corner from the Silver Dollar. We first noticed the car rocking, a male got out holding a big brown paper bag, and a long screwdriver sticking out of his right side rear pocket. The male had broken into the car and snatched out the stereo system. He noticed our car parked behind him. He got out and walked across the street, walking quickly toward Atlantic Avenue. I called it in, stating I was stopping the male suspect! I gave a location and needed backup, Tom drove halfway up the block letting me out in the middle of the street. The suspect saw me get out the car but didn't realize that I was the police because my uniform was under my coat, plus I was wearing my Stevie Wonder Hat. I grabbed him and threw him against the fence pulling the screw driver out his back pocket, placed him into hand-cuffs. An unknown male was walking by Twelve South Tavern front door entrance, when two males came running out the bar knocking the male down to the ground, they were part of the stake-out-team. I later realized that I needed to yell to them that I had the male in custody. That was not the male in question! Units came to my location, in the middle of the block, and transported the suspect into Detective Bureau for charges. Because I was the complainant, it was a done deal, so I thought. We picked up the orders of food, went back to City Hall, and I went into the Detective Bureau and started the paperwork for the arrest. The Captain came storming in with much attitude towards me, for going into the area, he said at roll call, "off limits". I tried to explain I had no knowledge of his order, to stay out of the area. I was given permission, by my supervisor to go because there was someone to cover for me, if I were to be needed, in processing a person being booked and placed in lockup. I didn't know if they trusted me on the streets or an innocent person was attacked by the stake out team, who was not, on top of their game having things under surveillance, but instead somewhere else. (tavern) I was lead to believe and realized, Jesus had my back and no harm would come to me, under His protection!

The same Captain, who was so unprofessional towards me for making the car stereo theft arrest, got a taste of his own medicine. This particular incident happened about two months later in mid-June, anyway I was put back on patrol, with a new partner. This person graduated from the Police Academy along with me. He had a "go get-them" type of attitude. I was just the opposite, I was more laid back and kept a strong focus on what was going on, I learned that from my Dad. We were dispatched to a loud music call, about 1:30 a.m. over on the Westside. The complaint was unknown to us. We went to the nineteen hundred block of Magellan Avenue, where there was a crowd of people, young adults standing around. They were some sitting on the porch as we pulled up. Things seemed to be orderly, and quiet. We could hear no loud music being played. I wanted to get out the patrol car and speak with the host of the party, my partner who was driving slowed up and stopped in front of the house for a moment and then pulled off from that location. He gave communication the disposition of the call "No loud music, people gathered not disorderly, no action taken." We were fifty-four (in-service), something was up with this partner, I didn't like it. It seemed he would drive to the Sea Wall known for couples making out (sexual activity), drinking or fishing, a place to park and talk about things. It was like he was trying to catch a particular person in the wrong. This is where he drove to after clearing the previous loud music call. He made a stop towards a parked car in the Seawall area. A couple was in the back-seat, the woman was on her back. My partner had knocked on the rear window trying to get the unknown male's attention who had his head placed between. . .: the male wouldn't raise his head, but signaled us by motioning his hand to get away. He told us to leave him alone, the car was not reported stolen which we had already known. The woman sat up and was facing me, the light from my flashlight shined in her face. I recognized who she was, and I told my partner let's go now! She was not the prettiest woman in the face area, but she had one heck of a physical shape. Put it this way, the lady may have been sixty but she had a body like someone in their early twenties. I recognized her from seeing her working at different stores in Atlantic City. We then were told by communication to see the Deputy Commissioner, at his Ohio Avenue address right away! Within ten minutes we were at his home, the Deputy Commissioner walked outside of his home as we pulled up to it. Then he confronted us, wanting to know why the loud music was never cut off, (The party is over) and ordered my partner to go back to the party to shut it down or write summonses for court, and to make arrest if necessary. As we confronted the party it began to shut down. People were driving off in their cars and the lights were on inside the house. I wrote down their names, the owner of the house who threw the party. I expressed to them we didn't want to come back, because three strikes and you're out. Let's not have that to happen; it took about twenty minutes to clear from the order given by the Deputy Public Safety Commissioner to go back to Magellan Avenue. The next request or order was to meet him at City Hall, we cleared and so we did.

The Deputy Commissioner showed up unexpectedly catching the Captain, that had a problem with me because I was in an off-limit area, (Silver Dollar) he was caught sleeping in his office, feet up on the desk and the door was closed but not locked, the Deputy Public Safety Commissioner walked in on him. I overheard him asking the Captain, "what the hell is going on, you were sleep, feet on the desk and the door shut not locked, listen clown," he said, "anyone who comes in this police department for whatever reason, this door better be open if you are in here, so they can see who is in charge of the shift (patrol). I can, and will whip your behind, take your badge and gun, only for you to report for disciplinary actions that will be filed against you on Monday." The Captain was mad, very nervous and he was an apple red showing his fear of the Deputy Commissioner. Some people don't realize what goes around most of the time comes back around to you; it's a vicious circle. This Deputy Public Safety Commissioner held the good-ole boys network from covering their butts. The Deputy Commissioner, was not scared of those boys, at all!

The Deputy Public Safety Commissioner was on a roll. He threatened my partner for not performing his duty on our previous call, about the loud music. They were standing in the Captain's office as I was walking by heading toward the men's room. I was using the urinal when the Deputy Commissioner came up, beside me using the other urinal, I started smiling, at myself thinking of what he told that Captain, and now he is going to get a taste of his own medicine. I told the Deputy Commissioner, I just started working on the streets and was paired off with my partner who was in question with me trying to understand his attitude what makes him tick. I did what I had to do, not to become a mark man among co-workers.

The change of government was passed by the Atlantic City voting public. It went from a Commissioner Form to a Council Form of Government. The Commissioner of Finance was the First Black State Banking Official. He was an active member of Omega Psi Phi Fraternity, Upsilon Alpha Chapter, of Atlantic City, and as a (side-note) his wife was my fifth grade teacher, Horace Bryant was his name! I viewed this change, the form of government, as a power move, to change the head of Public Safety!

The Deputy Public Safety Commissioner was transferred back to the Police Department, was promoted to sergeant, assigned to the Detective Bureau four-to-twelve p.m. shift. I whole-heartedly believe the change of the Public Safety was due because men of color were in charge of it. The good ole boy net-work will always be around even in this present time. One day, fairness "for all" will be instituted to the men and women in the ranks of the Police Force, an inside track in having an influence on policies and rules that affect the member of the force! I'm pretty sure this is a national issue reaching all Police department everywhere that there are Police. Administrations.

So it was in their best interest, to have the change in government, I believe all stops were pulled out, meaning some police officers did what they had to do to get this measure passed, resulting in getting those two Black men out of office. The next mayor of Atlantic City was voted into office in 1982.

I graduated from Stockton State College, in May of 1983 with a Bachelor of Arts degree, in Criminal Justice. My degree proves to me that I had the discipline to continue over eight years, from graduating from Atlantic City High School to receiving my four year degree. After all, I could have put it on the back-burner in my life. Also I can learn from anyone who does not have the same level education that I have. Again, it may have taken me eight total years to receive my college degree, but I got it! I didn't owe any student loans, please keep me in your Grace walking with you, giving, Jesus the highest praise!

The sitting mayor who came into office in 1982 was arrested by the state on corruption charges. After a plea deal, he was sentenced to fifteen years in Federal Prison.

The first Black person elected as Mayor of Atlantic City, New Jersey was in 1984. He was a Republican. This City was known to be Democratic. This person was an educator in the school district of Atlantic City, with over twenty-four years of service; he was an administer in the public school system just before being elected as the city's first Black Mayor. Lastly, he was a member of Omega Psi Phi. Fraternity. Inc, in which many have been called and in fact few are chosen to join the ranks of Omega Psi Phi Fraternity, Inc.

During this time of the shakeup of the government in the City, I was transferred to Bravo Platoon's four to twelve midnight shift; I was placed in booking and detention (turnkey). My responsibilities were to take head count of male incarcerated prisoners, order meals that were needed for dinner always adding five to what was actually needed and prepared those males to be transported out to the County Jail. At this time inmates, would not be in our facility over seven days normally, they were also allowed fifteen minutes visiting time for those incarcerated, with family or friends. Anyone that came to visit must have proper I.D.; a warrant check was made, if that person had an outstanding warrant that showed up on N.C.I.C.! This was known as National Crime Information Center, person would be placed under arrest and put into lockup.

One time we (team booking and detention) were getting the shipment of about seven males ready for transportation to Mays Landing. One of the males being transported was charged with the murder of a second degree; he was with a girl over at the Pitney Village and she was shot and died. He was charged, claiming it was an accident. This incident happened inside an apartment on a couch in a Pitney

Village Public Housing Unit. His brother came to visit, before he would be shipped out, the visiting brother had an outstanding warrant on the N.C.I.C. computer bank. He too, was immediately arrested! In the processing area for those about to be incarcerated, as he was taking out his belt, taking off his hat and sneaker shoe strings a search of his person, packages of C.D.S. (Control Dangerous Substance) was found. Additional charges were filed against him. We handcuffed both brothers together for the transportation process to Mays Landing County Jail. As we were walking out to the Police van, a group of girls (four girls) started calling the murder suspect names. Yelling and screaming, he projected as if he were a V.I.P. (very important person) with Police Protection. His chest was out and his walk was as if he were a king; the girls made him think he was a rock star. Once on arrival to the County, the brothers were uncuffed, searched, and told by the intake officers that because of the charges, he would be placed in protective custody for the murder of a female. He was led away crying, and looking back at his brother with the look, why me? What a turnaround from the rear of City Hall (group of girls) to being led away.

I had met through a mutual friend, while working on Charlie Platoon inside as turnkey a friend, that eventually became my wife. The young lady who introduced us had the same first name as my mother. After sometime later, a long distance relationship, we decided to marry. We found a house in Pleasantville, made settlement on February 2th, moved in on February 6th; she brought her things down from New York City, and we married on Valentines Day February 14, 1985 on the anniversary of my parents!

Chapter Seven

"Many Are Called, Few Chosen"

About four months, I, with eleven other college degree men, underwent the challenge of pledging Omega Psi Phi Fraternity, Inc. Graduate Chapter, Upsilon Alpha of Atlantic City, New Jersey. It was about a six-week pledge program, and something I wanted to achieve for many of years. My pledge line was known as the "Dynamic Dozen," and I was known as, "Deputy Dog!"

I soon was placed in Foot Patrol on 4 p.m. to midnight, Bravo of Safe Streets Unit, (Walking Patrol). My normal Foot Patrol area was the Boardwalk, or the north side of North Carolina Avenue to Kentucky Avenue, Adriatic to Arctic Avenue. One day just before roll call, the Desk Sergeant told me they wanted me in the Mayor's office right away. I went up to the Mayor's office and spoke with Captain Byard another Que, who was in charge of Police Community Relation. He told me to disregard the request at that time, I made it back downstairs before roll call. Another member of the "Good Ole Boys" network among the policymaking and treatment of certain officers, was our shift commander that day. He asked me "Who the hell do you think you are reporting upstairs to the Mayor's office without going through chain of command?". I tried to explain to him I was informed and instructed by Sgt. Murray to report upstairs, and once informed I was no longer needed, I returned back downstairs for roll call. Three days later, I was asked by some superior police official, if I could drive the Mayor to Philadelphia Airport the next morning and bring him back to the City about twenty four hours later. I agreed to make the journey!

I was invited to a close circuit fight party. It was held on my sister's birthday; I had to wait for her to come home to give her a present that I bought for her, and cut some cake that my mother had made for her. It was more or less a small family gathering.

I went to a liquor store and bought a case of beer. At the fight party was about twenty-five people gathered, some casino workers, gym personnel, and cops who had membership. It was a Mike Tyson fight, who was on top of the world during this time. There was plenty of food, liquor, conversation and coke. I'm not talking about soda! Going through the changes that had been placed on me, I went for it! We are only human, on a job made up from people in society, everything in our society can be a reflection on the police force whole. It felt normal being present at the gathering.

I was out one night with my wife, and we stopped at the Silver Dollar for a light snack. There was a suspicious male that entered the tavern/restaurant, who was making patrons very uncomfortable.

The male wandered over to our table, placed a gold chain on it and said "Give me seventy-five dollars and the chain will be yours." I went to hand it back to him, but my wife being from the Apple, told him that he must be crazy! At that time he had called her a "b" and grabbed it out of her hand, leaning towards her as though he was going to strike her, at that time I drew my gun. My gun's safety, released itself, and got snagged on my sweater. A shot rang out, I put a whole in the wall where he was standing, and the male looked down and ran out the tavern, leaving his jacket. I immediately asked was anyone hurt! The tavern was crowed, no one was hurt! I went out the tavern and tried to find him. I looked up the block to corner of M.L.K. Avenue, where I saw him talking to a police unit, all of sudden they rolled up on me, shotgun pointing, the suspect came running up the street at full speed, saying to the officers, that the man right there! The officers recognized me having a newly grown beard! I said "Excuse me officers!", as I walk toward the male, I threw him against the police car, showing him my badge and I.D. I am the police I told him! I went inside the tavern spoke to the manager, who didn't want any problems from the suspect. I paid my tab, and left a tip for our waitress. I took the male his jacket that he left behind, no complaints, no arrest, and I allowed him to leave. I remembered that last time what happened to me because of an arrest around that area. Once I got home I called my captain at home, I explained what had happened. He instructed me to write a report and submit it to him at work the next day, and I did. Captain

Duncan got transferred to head Internal Affairs; my case was one of his first as commander of that unit. Internal Affairs on completion of the investigation, it had suggested that I get a thirty-day suspension without pay. Captain "D" intervened by suggesting I only get half the time of suspension fifteen days without pay. I agreed and that was the punishment that was dealt to me. I, then, informed the tavern manager to take legal action to have repair work completed because of my incident, in which he did. At this time they made a "special beat" just for me, the only time it was patrolled (foot) was by me, 4 p.m. to midnight, and no officers were assigned to that beat, on my days off. This beat was on M.L.K. Boulevard, from Baltic Avenue to the Westside School Complex (M.L.K.), and is also known as Martin Luther King Complex. That was eight blocks away from Baltic Avenue. It was basically a residential area, having public housing, Stanley Holmes Village and some private family dwellings. Across from the school complex was another privately owned apartment complex. On this street lived the current business administrator, who would sometimes sit on his porch, reading his newspapers. We would acknowledge one another most of the times; the other times, he would be deep in reading or thought.

One great lady that live on my beat, always had something for me to eat or drink, a place where I could get out of the weather elements if necessary. Her son is also a law enforcement official in the Sheriff's Office. Ron and I met and became close friends, and still are even to this day! He can relate to people; they give him a heads-up with information on people. Those who trust him, have high respect for him even lawbreakers that he has arrested. We both were on the same page in this matter, having the respect and trust of many people in doing our job to protect and serve. How would you want to be treated if the shoes were on the other foot?

On a different date while patrolling my designated area, I was talking with Doug, who was driving a one man patrol unit. He and several other units were dispatched to the five hundred block North Tennessee Avenue because shots were fired. We were only three blocks away, I got in his unit and we responded. We were the first unit to arrive along with a street supervisor. The three of us, went up three flights of stairs. A male was lying in his doorway face up and his eyes were open, he had been shot. I went back downstairs (as more patrol units were arriving) people started to gather on the street, outside the apartment building. We needed witnesses, with information to this crime or later come forward with information in privacy. Yellow crime scene tape (now a homicide) was erected.

The victim was a former Atlantic City Firemen, who had a brother that was a police officer and their father was a former Captain with the department. It was later learned that the victim had come home carrying shopping bags in his hand and a group of juveniles was blocking the door not allowing him to gain entry into his apartment building. He asked them to move out the way, he was struggling with his packages. An argument ensued, some physical contact was made, with one of the juveniles involved. The juvenile that was charged with the crime actually lived on the same level across from the victim's apartment. The supervisor had no problem with me leaving my assigned area of patrol without permission to backup Doug, to whom I was talking with. The second patrol unit was on the scene, giving additional coverage for him, the supervisor. About three weeks later, again I was holding a conversation with Doug, on M.L.K. Boulevard. Several patrol units were dispatched to the Public Housing Complex ("six-bedrooms") located on North Carolina and Adriatic Avenue. There were several 911 calls with the statement, "Man with a gun". I got into Doug's patrol vehicle and we sped off to the call. It was about eight units that responded to the call! A male approximately nineteen years old was caught in the rear of the housing complex. He was searched! There was a hostler found in the waist band of his pants. His attitude with police got him arrested! He was handcuffed and led away to a patrol unit. City Hall, Detective Bureau, one is on his way! I was walking in the rear, left side of the suspect along with officers; it was a crowd of people gathering because of the excitement, police units, lights flashing, K-9 dogs, and the nice weather, to cap it off. All of sudden, I was struck with a glass bottle, on top of my head; it apparently was thrown down from a rooftop of the complex. I felt my head and blood started pouring out, along with the suspect, we ran to a police unit. I was rushed to the Atlantic Medical Center, where I received four stitches. I was in a waiting line, to be X-rayed for possible head injuries. I was the next person to go in for X-rays, when a male was on a stretcher and was placed in front of me. He was hit with a baseball bat at the same Housing Project, Six Bedrooms. He had received twenty-four stitches, to close his head wound. The victim was from Pleasantville, went to visit a girl in the housing project. He was walking out of the complex, when someone ran up behind him, on the street and struck him in the back of the head with a aluminum baseball bat. Hearing and seeing this person being wheeled by, I calmed down and started praying for the victim of the bat attack. I thanked God, because my injuries could have been a lot worse. The person that was responsible for my injuries was later identified by a family informant. I served him some street corner just-us, just him and I. I was out on workman's compensation for about three weeks.

During my absence for my injuries to my head, a co-worker was pull to the red carpet in an investigation dealing with substance abuse, among the ranks. He told what he knew about. My name being mentioned, I used at that fight party. My urine was tested, it came back negative. I informed the investigators how on October 14th, 1981 after the fact my stress level/situation was never addressed, especially with direct contact to it. Drinking was the beginning which developed for some into a stress and counseling was provided to all on a whole. Example: If a person attended a school/college and dies from an incident, counseling was offered to all who knew the victim. Was it because, I admitted my thoughts of not having any treatment that was not justified, or was it pure racism. I felt no one honestly cared; they had their own interest in themselves.

I returned to work from my three week injury leave and was informed in order to keep my job, I had to attend and complete a a twenty-eight day program. It was covered by medical insurance, Blue Cross & Blue Shield of New Jersey. It cost one thousand dollars a day. I wanted my job, and I love my job and the people I served. I had admitted, in the pass of being human at the fight party, I would be sent off to this Rehab Hospital. The person who was the, "Go between" was a former K-9 officer with the Atlantic City Police Department. During this time he was in charge of the Tow Lot, he was terminated from his police position for allegedly discharging his weapon at another male who was visiting his girlfriend down in Longport. The go between girlfriends was a high up person in the Public Safety Office (years back) for the City of Atlantic City. The Business Administrator's family member had a personal problem, and their casino job afforded them the time to seek help for their problems. This was the same drug rehab, twelve step program. The name of my hospital was called Carrier, located near Princeton University.

They took blood work and urine samples for all to be admitted to the facility. My results came back negative. Some officers "partied" one last time before leaving to attempt their new change in life, which caused their results to be off the chart with substance abuse recorded in their system. I had to stay in order to keep my job, and complete a twenty eight day program. I was placed in psychological ward; this would justify the billing to the insurance and have job protection, because I was treated for post trauma resulting from the shooting incident!

I was allowed off the hospital grounds (pass) on visiting day, my first seven days was on Sunday, and I was granted to be signed out and returned by 5 p.m. Most patients must stay on grounds at least three weeks before being granted a pass!

This **rehab hospital was** *the* top shelf or Betty Ford's east coast cousin, one thousand a day, not including medication if needed. It's not important where you go for help, but asking your spiritual higher power for acceptance and guidance. Some of the doctors were associated with Princeton University, not far away - some serving on its Board and Medical panel. Some of the patients had jobs in teaching, administrators, lawyers, nurses, car dealership owners, state employees, and police officers. Bottom line, those are the people with great insurance coverage. My personal belief, to be able to turn this page in your life or starting a new chapter in your life, one must put Jesus first above all things, and pray for protection. Also to put the hate out of your heart start loving yourself! You must do this for your- self, no other reason will work stay in prayer and Jesus does all but fail!

I was allowed to go into other wards to play cards, watch television, and socialize with others in the evening after dinner usually. Although my ward would be on lockdown (8 p.m.) normally during the changing of the nurse's shift about 10 p.m., I would be waiting by the door to re-enter into my ward. I helped with some of the patience, that were unwilling to take their medicines, by using a kind word or saying something positive that they did doing the day. I mentioned and made them feel great about themselves, and took charge of the task at hand, cooperating with the medical staff.

A week before being discharged from the rehab, my medical counselor (Ph.D.), the "go between" person and I met in her office for the purpose of structuring an aftercare program to follow when discharged back into the world. My counselor suggested that I attend one N.A. meeting a week, but if I chose to go to more meetings, it would be my decision. She stated because I had no substance in my urine or my blood work, I was treated for post-trauma and that it was no need to meet for a required four meetings of N.A. for the police department. The "go between" person, got real loud and very unprofessional. He demanded I be placed on a mandatory four-week program, it got real nasty between the both of them. She told him she had the degrees hanging on the wall and what she said was law. The "Go Between" lost his control, and caused me to pick-up the phone and call for help. Security rushed in and escorted him out of her office!

The next week, a group of us were discharged after completing a twenty-eight day program at Rehab facility. I was again transferred (treated like a ping pong ball) this time Juvenile Bureau! I was put on the 4 p.m. shift to midnight, it was a total surprise this was hap-pening, but when I thought about it, the Public Safety especially the

Police Department had no fair, responsible leadership to its members and the City at hand!

During my first week in juvenile, I wore my uniform, and held the title of detective. Having that title, your pay would increase after a year in that unit, but you should keep your uniform because at any time, you could be ordered to report back into uniform no "If or buts"! I chose to wear my issued uniform for several reasons. I wanted to learn the paper work, procedures and names of juveniles, and other agencies involved in matters dealing with youth offenders. Harborfields, a county juvenile detention center, basically housed them, until they went before a judge. The Division of Youth & Family Services dealt with family, child abuse matters, or the protection of a child.

The dress clothes I had were not brought for me to run, climb, and jump or even struggle with someone being placed under arrest. The sergeant that I was with on the shooting call on Tennessee Avenue was the supervisor on my shift. We had no problem, he knew I was capable of doing my job. He later was promoted to Captain and became the Juvenile Bureau Unit Commander. Another sergeant was transferred in to take the outgoing supervisor's position, who is now a Captain. This sergeant and my dad have history together working on the force together. He had a great attitude towards people. The sergeant had a look and listen approach. He wouldn't let you hurt yourself, he would do anything from self-destruction, for anyone under his command. The Mayor's Office called down to the Juvenile office and requested I report to the office when I arrived at work that day. When I was informed of the request, I asked the sergeant to company me up to the office and he did. The Mayor wanted to know why I would not wear a dress shirt and tie to work in the Juvenile Bureau. "All Omega men must do that". I told him on this clock, I'm the police. What little good stuff I had to wear, I didn't want to mess it up on the streets. I am the only person working in my household, therefore the bills fall on me. Hoping my wife's postal transfer would follow through, as promised by a certain council member on City Council.

The Mayor, in front of my supervisor said, "Nigger get out my office!" We both got up and left, outside his office door and we both looked at each other shaking our heads. I got some things together that I could wear and felt comfortable working in; I used my clip on blue uniform issued tie.

One evening working in the juvenile office about 6 p.m., when a friend of my Dad's came in the juvenile office, Mr. Bobby had gone into the detective bureau and the detectives referred him to our unit. Juveniles burglarized his home, possibly his sons' friends. There was a dog tied up blocking the entrance to the rear door in the backyard. The dog was about two years old. It appeared to be a big aggressive dog, again big in size. There was no forced entry into the home. The backdoor was unlocked, and the things taken were watches, rings, and a loaded nine millimeter pistol in its case. The gun was licensed, the incident happened in three hundred block of Drexel Avenue. I volunteered to get involved, this was the first time I worked in any case, outside of my office. I found out what juveniles were responsible for his theft. My investigations lead me to a house, on Congress Avenue, where one of the juveniles lived with his family. The accused ringleader juvenile was not home. I spoke with his uncle who was the only adult home at the time. I made a promise, that if I get the gun back before the end of my midnight shift, nobody goes to jail. It was about 7pm and time was moving on. If I didn't get these items back, may god protect you from me? I'm going to be all up in it, it won't be pretty! The uncle promised, I would hear from him within a few hours, one way or the other. About 11;15p.m. that night, I got a call to drive up to Downey Place in the Inlet. The package, which was in question, would be handed over to me at that location. I went right away, I snatched up B.A. (partner), he let me out the car, and I walked up the small street. It was a poorly lit street and had numerous row homes ready to be torn down. About three juveniles came climbing out of one, of the houses. I instructed them to walk toward me, wave their hands in the air. One had a dark leather package in his hand. He placed the package on the ground and they walked away from it. I walked over to it and picked the package case up. I opened it; the weapon, a nine millimeter, two clips loaded, some jewelry and a watch, were inside the leather case. I notified my co-worker; who drove around and picked me up. I had communication to have all units in the area to clear, be safe and thanks for their help! A gun was off the streets, not to fall into foul play. Mr. Bobby was notified; he picked the package up at 11:53 p.m. This case was now officially closed!

Chapter Eight

"Never Let Go Of Jesus' Unchanging Hands!"

Near to the date of being assigned from patrol to plain clothes in the Juvenile Bureau, when an officer would receive a two percent increase in pay. I decided to take the exam to become a firefighter. I already had a four percent increase on my base pay for earning my Bachelor of Arts degree. As a fireman working four days on, and four days off is the ticket, a job that I knew I could handle. The written part of the exam was pass or fail, which I passed. The physical part is based on your time completing an obstacle course. Your score determined your rank on the list to be eligible. You must be long-winded and mentally sharp using small advantages in your favor to increase your time of completing the course. The Vocans, a group of Atlantic City firefighters who are black men that held training sessions for any person interested in learning the procedures in the physical exam. During this time, no females were serving as firefighters. The Vocans sponsor training sessions at the

State Armory located at New York and Absecon Boulevard (Route 30). A large crowd of applicants took advantage of this opportunity; practices were held in the evening from 6 p.m. until 9 p.m. I trained on the side, running on the Boardwalk. I got up to one and half miles in one direction, a total of three miles every other day, pumping iron/weights. I rested on Sunday! I never will forget the night of the official test at the State Armory. State Civil Service Officials were present, armed with their stop watches, keeping time on the applicants. Robert Bob Green (now retired) Captain, a recruitment officer ran outside behind me. I was so exhausted, I gave it my all and didn't hear him calling me. I had stopped and he had caught up to me. "Wesley, are you a veteran?" I replied no, with my score and being a veteran, would have placed me near the very top of the entry list! I could have been considered for employment A.C.F.D.

One of my neighbors living in Bungalow Park was the first African American chief of the Atlantic City Fire Department. His in-laws lived directly across the street from my parents' home. His father-in-law was an Omega-man (Que) from way back! Yes, this gentleman had a great conversation that he shared with me how he had to struggle to climb to make the rank of chief. His wife and my mother have the same first name! I will talk about one of the many conversations we held later on in this book! One night, my partner in the Juvenile Bureau and I went to "White House Sub" shop on our dinner break. We were only a couple of bites away from finishing our sub and soda when we heard the call from communication sending numerous patrol units into the Back Maryland Avenue, the eight hundred block area regarding unknown trouble. The first unit arriving moments later, found a male victim assaulted and was hit in the head with an object. Lying in blood on the ground, just on the outer perimeter of the housing units, we were called because juveniles (suspects) were involved in the investigation.

The victim had ties with a Philadelphia professional sports team. I can't remember which one, but I knew his brother or maybe father was working for the organization. The victim was walking to the casino right up the street that sits on the bayside of the State Marina, where boats are docked. We responded right away. I was driving our unmarked vehicle; I dropped B.A.. off about a half block from the incident. He walked up the street and blended into the crowd of hundreds who have gathered. No one notice B.A. presence in the crowd, he was the police. People were talking and information was being gathered; he overheard who was involved and what they had on and where they ran. B.A.. had gotten all the information, a couple of apartments down from where he was standing. After B.A. called for additional units to meet him for further information, we surrounded the apartment and it was surrounded. B.A.. and I knocked on the front door, and the suspect opened the door, wearing the shirt with blood stains splattered on it. He was brought in for questioning and later picked out of a photo lineup. He was identified and charged with the crime. "Faith" had a big part in me choosing to resign from the police department. I would like to share the incident that took me over the edge and the treatment that was not justified, but I was subject to deal with it! Thank You, Jesus for keeping and holding on to me!

I was riding with a different partner in patrol. Roscoe and I were in a two-man car. About six units were sent on a call, "man with a gun" at Florida and Fairmont Avenues. It was a neighborhood tavern, the complainant met us on arrival, standing in front of the corner tavern. The accused pulled a handgun on the complainant, the incident involving a woman. The accused lived above the tavern, and the entry to his apartment was from the rear of the tavern. We "Police" positioned ourselves, guns drawn including a couple shot-guns pointed at the door. I was standing on the side of the door, we knocked on the door, saying Police! Moments later, the door opened but the hinges to the door were on the wrong side. The door opened and the accused was standing at the bottom of the steps. The lights were on at the top of the stairs only seeing his silhouette at the bottom of the stairs. He was holding a long barrel hand-gun pointed downward. I smelled alcohol strongly, he didn't see the other units because the door blocked his vision. I took action, knowing what I was put through before, when discharging my weapon on the Bridge. Within seconds I holstered my weapon, I knocked him down to the bottom of the steps. I grabbed the barrel of the gun, keeping it pointed away from me, striking him across his shoulder blade several times, until he finally released his weapon. The other backup units came running over to assist, but the narrow stairwell prevented them in reaching him because I was on top of him striking him with my Maglight (flashlight). I heard the sound of the pellets sliding in the weapon barrel, as I took control of it. I could have shot this man to death over a pellet gun. I really got heated, I was told by several officers "Wes walk down to the corner, there's a fire hydrant opened, go cool off or cut it off Wes." I did walk away, but I was very, very upset! The accused suspect was lucky to still be alive! He was some relative of a construction/ demolition company owner. He received no jailed time for his charges and putting me in that mode. May the force be with you, it was over with me, That was man's powers, but Jesus had me; His force is awesome in my life, as you will see as you continue to read my journey, in my walk through life, holding on to faith being one of his children; "Let's roll!"

Due to this previous incident, "A man with a gun," on Wednesday, August 13th, 1986, I was ordered to see a psychologist in Philadelphia, Pennsylvania. I was ordered to report August 21st, 1986. Just getting out of rehab, under a year, having no justified reason to report to a psychologist for behavioral or treatment. I was to drive myself, to Philadelphia in my own car. I was not able to because my wife needed our vehicle to get to her job in Belmar, New Jersey, about a fifty-five minutes ride for her district post office employment. There was a conflict again but one gets accustomed to it.

On my last night at work, B.A. and I had been transferred out of the Juvenile Bureau and placed into patrol unit. We were walking in a high crime area, with public housing projects, a few bars, and lots of people that seemed to have no hope with the struggle of life. My last call that night was, 225 North Virginia Avenue, fourteenth floor, a domestic.

My Dad, B.A., and I were talking when the call was given to us. My dad said "It sounds like your uncle's apartment." On arrival, B.A. and I responded, taking the elevator, when we got off, a female was standing there bleeding cursing at someone unknown to us. She wanted him arrested and put out of the apartment, so she could return to the inside. Looking at a blood trail from the elevator on the wall and floor, back-up was requested and our weapons were drawn as we followed it to the apartment door. We knocked on the door, announcing police. The door was unlocked; we entered and a male had his back to us. He was attempting to mop up the blood on the floor. When he turned around, it was my uncle, who was bleeding heavily from his arm. We holstered our weapons and I went to his aid. The woman came in with backup officers requesting he be arrested. I asked him to get his lease, to see whose name the apartment was in. It was in his name. I told him get to the hospital for medical attention and to sign a complaint on her. "Tell them just what you told me; you asked her to leave and she refused. Picking up a kitchen knife she tried to stab you, you defended yourself the best you knew how, trying to put her out the apartment unit; remember you are handicapped and had been drinking, and she wouldn't let you near the phone to call the police."

The next morning, I was called home by a detective who was familiar with the above situation. He was being pressured by someone in the Housing Authority to have my uncle removed for the numerous domestic calls and most recently the blood smeared all over the elevator, hallway walls and floor. They wanted him out. The charges must be prosecuted! The detective wanted to know, why I didn't place him under arrest. I told him, the facts and what he promised he would do countersigning a complaint. However, my uncle never came in to sign a complaint.

I told him, I planned to resign as of today and that I would submit my resignation to the chief of police on August 18th, 1987. At approximately 10 a.m., my father and I went up to the chief's office to turn in the following items, a bulletproof vest, badge, police I.D. card, one service revolver 357 magnum, tac radio with charger, and a letter of why I chose to resign.

I informed them to "allow the record to reflect that I am resigning in response to the fact that repeatedly and without justification; I have been ordered by non-medically trained police department personnel to undergo psychiatric evaluation. Specifically, I was ordered to be evaluated most recently on August 21st, 1986. None of these orders have been based on medical conclusions, but were instead arbitrary and capricious acts taking the form of harassment. Indeed, I have written documentation to support this viewpoint. Also note I was evaluated in the most recent past resulting in a finding that I do not suffer from any form of mental disorder! In conclusion, I thank you for your anticipated cooperation. In the beginning there was only the chief and his secretary, who was sitting in the outer office. By the time my father and I left someone had called for additional police to respond to his office because an emotional employee was in the chief's office. About seven uniformed police responded, I threw in the towel. It was like you can't, we have many "more obstacles for you to jump". I prayed to Jesus keep on protecting me, and to have mercy on those that seem to be caught up in something that they think is bigger than Jesus! (Themselves!)

Chapter Nine

"HE'S My Everything"

Several months later, after separating from my wife, I started to work for Showboat Casino in security from midnight to 8 a.m. The night before I started at Showboat, the Deltas and the Ques hosted our first Winter Wonderland Ball. We packed the place, filling their biggest Ballroom in town. The Mississippi Room was "On and Jumping!"

At roll call my first night at the Boat, I was introduced to the crew, some who knew me, congratulated me on a successful affair held the night before. A few supervisors were also impressed because so many People of Color of all ages were dressed in a formal fashion with the holiday spirit, and there was not one incident needing security or police. The following years, I had no problem in selling four or five tables along with several hundred in patrons for our souvenir booklet for our Ball. I have met some great people who work, gamble or just pass thru from time to time. Some are still in contact with me to this day. During the five year I worked at showboat, I came across, an employee in the cafeteria, a friend who attended Stratford Military Academy with me, back in the day. Curtis and I sang in the cadet choir. He gave me a group picture that we had taken while at the Academy. Yes, at Showboat, I had some fond memories and great times!

While working at Showboat, I developed Diabetes. One day after the fourth annual Delta and Que (Omega Psi Phi) Winter Wonderland Ball, I was posted at the front entrance to the casino floor. My main duty was to stop possible underage gamblers' entry to the floor, answer questions, and give directions for certain locations for different activities in the casino complex. My post was next to the men's room; not knowing, my sugar was high kept me using the men's room and drinking water, from the water fountain nearby. The supervisor that introduced me to the security shift, was standing off at a distance looking at my behavior – men's room, water, men's room, water, men's room, and then water! He called the casino podium, to have an available security guard report to the casino floor entrance to take my post. I was ordered by him to go to the Medical Station, to have myself checked-out, because of my behavior. The nurse on duty insisted I get something to eat, I took my hour break and I did eat and drink something.

Later on that night, just about an hour before I was to get off, I was asked by a patron which way was the Boardwalk. I looked up to point with my hand in the direction of the outer hallway that paralleled the casino floor, the lights were flashing on top of the slot machines for several reasons. Patron needing change, slot machines needing their hoppers filled (coins put in) to pay the patron playing the machine or large jackpots paid by cash in hand by a slot attendant. The Casino floor flashing lights on top of the slot machine, hundreds of lights scattered, I was totally confused in which way to direct them, some other employee to whom I was standing next to provide the patron the assistance that they requested. Three hours later, I was standing at my original post by the men's room, and it started all over again. I immediately was sent to the Medical Station again, this time the nurse requested I report to the Atlantic City Medical Center Emergency Room right away. I called my Dad to pick me up and had a co-worker Mike Sullivan drove my car to my house when he got off at twelve midnight. I was in the emergency room for about five and a half hours before being seen by a doctor. It was realized then, that the wrong procedure was given to me. I would have to wait an additional hour and twenty minutes, changing of the shift to see a doctor about my condition. I refused and walked out and I was off from Showboat, for the next two days.

My father got me up out of bed, at 6 a.m. and drove me to his doctor. I was in his office within a half hour later, he sent me directly to admission for a stay at the hospital. They had to get my sugar under control, I was now a member of the "Sugar Hill Gang". (Diabetic)

I was out from work for thirty days not including days off, a whole new lifestyle was on its way! I was discharged from the hospital three days after Christmas of 1993. I wouldn't celebrate it with my family, with gifts, laughter, and memorable moments until January 5th, 1994, the day we buried my mom in 1988. I celebrated it in my hospital bed thinking of my mother, who was in Heaven, and praying for friends, families, and those who don't know Jesus. Christmas day in the hospital was the pits, involving a number of arguments, people visiting with their relatives discussing faults, and what should have been done to avoid their stay in the hospital, and the list goes on! Because of the amount of time being out of work, I applied and received City Welfare until my temporary disability unemployment kicked in. I was also granted food stamps, which was a help, thanks to a city caseworker, Mrs. Lyons who knew of my situation that shared with my father what I should do in getting back into the saddle of life, and that was working. The day I received my full payment of city welfare I also received three checks from temporary disability unemployment. I handed my check back over to city welfare, later learning I could have kept it. But when Jesus has you, there is no need to worry!

When I finally returned to work from my medical leave from developing diabetes, during mid-February of 1994, I was walking the casino floor near the main entrance when a person grabbed twelve one hundred dollar bills from a casino slot winner and ran out the front entrance. Security officers were in close pursuit, as I ran out the front entrance doors. The suspect was seen running across Showboat property. Our mobile Security Jeep pulled up and two of us got in with the assigned driver and took off after the fleeing suspect. He eventually started walking up Congress Avenue from Atlantic Avenue; we were parallel on Massachusetts Avenue and had him in sight. He started walking toward Walt's Bar located on Massachusetts and Grammercy Avenues. We had our command center call police, and have them meet us at Walt's bar. The suspect took off his outer jacket and laid it down near a street pole outside the entrance to Walt's bar. The police arrived in about a minute after being called. As the suspect got ready to go into Walt's, I along with the other two security officers exited our vehicle and walked toward him. He was looking at the police cars pulling up, and didn't see us approaching him from the opposite direction. I picked up his jacket that was lying on the ground and grabbed him by his arm. I had that grip and walked him over to the patrol car, where the police patted him down and placed him in the back seat of his patrol car. We returned to Showboat's main entrance, where the suspect was identified by the victim and he was placed under arrest and transported to the police station for processing. Jealously, I believe caused me my job at Showboat. I got along with people, patrons and most co-workers. I knew how to write reports, serious reports that involved Division of Gambling Enforcement (State Police) or the Atlantic City Police Department. I have been pulled from a standing post because, supervisors were unavailable to take a report. One time, a security guard in the patrol chart was hit in the parking garage (hit and run) by a patron, which was caught on surveillance cameras. The security officer stated he was not hurt but his cart had flipped on its side! A newly promoted female officer, who was now a sergeant on the same shift and did not like the respect that was given to me by others. I didn't want her position. She was the same supervisor who submitted the wrong count in medical leave time, which caused me to be placed with no sick time left. I would have had to work about a year in order to start having sick time again. I offered to pay the time back so I could have time if needed to take off. That was rejected by Showboat security management. This particular supervisor started me on money pickup about fifteen minutes late one day, I had to go to Redemption Booths and Cashier Booth surveillance cameras were on my every move. Rushing to get caught up with time, a trashcan had a smoldering fire in it. I called it in, and several slot attendants had brought over some coin cups filled with water. We poured it into the can, extinguishing the problem. I finished on time and rushed to get to my next assignment. I walked into a restricted area and lighted up a cigarette, and a new security officer came in and joined me. Surveillance never called down on the phone that was stationed on the wall in the area. The supervisor accused me of smoking in a restricted area. The Eye in the Sky Team, witnessed what I had gone through and didn't think it was a problem. If so, I would have been notified by them, but wasn't. I was reported by her to her supervisor and called upstairs into the captain's office. She stated I was the "only person" smoking in the area; she put me under a lot of unnecessary stress. I'm human; I lost it, and called her out of her name and explained that it's all on tape and that I was not the only one smoking; and that the tape should be checked. I was told to calm down, to get something to eat, and to cool off. I did, and when I returned, they told me go home and call back later to see where I'll be posted the next day. I left walking out on my own, not escorted out by a security officer. I got home about one hour later! It was like a ton of bricks being lifted off of my shoulders. Yes, I needed my job, but I refused to work under conditions that were intentionally trying to stop me from being who I am.

Losing my job at Showboat Casino where I was employed for five years, the only casino I ever worked, made me hold on tighter to keeping my faith, realizing I had a lot on my plate, and I kept on keeping on. It was a loss to Showboat, a team player they had lost. I have met and worked with some remarkable people and patrons. I received a call, one evening from the security podium (casino floor) at Showboat from one of my former co-workers to see how I was doing. She asked me "Guess who's down here playing Black Jack."? I replied my father, and she said no. I said who? She replied "Emmet Smith", the receiver for the Dallas Cowboys, N.F.L., back-to-back Champs. I told her I didn't believe her, but at that very moment she told me that he walked by the podium. I said, put him on the phone. She said, she couldn't do that, but "I know if you had still been employed, you would have found a way to exchange some conversation with him." We spoke a little bit longer and then hung up. Two days later someone dropped an envelope in my mailbox; it was a picture of Emmet Smith sitting at the Five Dollar Black Jack Table.

It blew me away! I was thought of enough, to have someone take a photo from one department passed it to another and then dropped it off in my mailbox, at home unexpectedly! Wow!

With the growing responsibilities to my two son's and self, lack of employment with Showboat Casino Hotel, I applied to the City of Atlantic City, Public Safety and personnel for the State of New Jersey to see if I could be considered to be rehired. I believe it fell on deaf ears because of the cloud of the state corruption charges, now indictments following for those involved.

The hotel and casino workers that were the service providers for its guest, (union members) held a job action rally at Park-Place and the Boardwalk. It had gotten out of control, police did not do their sworn duty with Public Safety. Injuries and property damages were reported in the local newspaper. The troubled Mayor blamed the Police Chief for not handling it correctly and the Police Chief blamed the Mayor for not having funds for the overtime needed to deal with the union rally. Continuing to hold on to Jesus' unchanging hand, I've witness the changing of how the City official corruption cases were handled. Some officials got plea deals and others jail time. The beat goes on! I wonder what's next that will continue to hold the City down and back from being the 'Pearl" that it really is!

Chapter Ten

"The Mustard Seed"

O ne off season day in February, the temperature was well above normal for that part of the year. Mylenda and I on the Boardwalk with the boys. Chris was in the carriage, Wes 3rd was running and walking, looking at the water and seagulls. Unexpectedly the newly elected Mayor and his Chief of Staff, Ms. Kitty, was walking up to the Boardwalk as we were coming down the ramp. It seemed they were checking out the condition of the water in front and the B'walk. We were at the closed Hackney's Restaurant, on Main Avenue and Melrose. The newly elected Mayor had not been in office for ninety days. I was not in a rush, but wanted consideration for employment, not with the Police or Public Safety Departments. I would take any Blue Collar or a White Collar position. I asked him if that were possible; the Mayor stated, he would get back to me. His assistant Ms. Kitty, wrote my information down, to contact me of any possibilities of employment. My sons, their mother, and I headed for home.

The newly elected Mayor was on a weekly noted local radio talk show I had come across trying to find T.J.M.S. He was discussing his plans for the City. One of the topics he discussed was employment with the City. "An applicant must have no criminal record, a high school or a G.E.D, diploma and be a resident of the city." I had all three and a four year degree! I had not heard from Ms. Kitty. I called the radio station at the end of the program, I spoke with him off the air. The Mayor instructed me to contact his chief of staff, Ms.kitty. That Monday, the first business day, contact was made. I had no problems with having a physical that was given about a week later. Approximately several days later, I learned I had passed the physical exam. Shortly thereafter I was employed!

I was assigned to the City Welfare Office as a security guard. This was the same office that helped me when I was diagnosed being a diabetic from Showboat Casino.

My starting date was Monday, April 4, 1994. This was the anniversary of Martin Luther King Jr. being assassinated. Also the entrance to the office is on Tennessee Ave. the state which Dr. KING was assassinated in. I could talk so much more but at this time, I will not! I'm just happy to be working. The lady who was the director of City Welfare when I joined the team, shortly retired about a month after I started my employment.

A new Director of City Welfare was selected and he was a caseworker, who was promoted to be Director. He passed over his supervisors and became their boss. His mother, now (retired) requested several times for me to substitute her class, at New Jersey Avenue School. We developed a great relationship over the years. Early on, he noticed I was a team player. I would do, whatever that was needed for any staff worker to help keep City Welfare moving in the right direction, in serving the people who needed help.

This office was responsible for single people without children in their care, those returning from being incarcerated, or those waiting on unemployment to kick in, assisted them with travelers aid, a one way ticket purchase to get them back home, a one shot deal, after a caseworker validated information given to them to be verified to assist the client with getting back home. Also, I would help those needing help in filling out paperwork or application for assistance. I would make photo copies if needed, applicants kept original copies of documents, and photo copies passed on to their caseworkers to open up their cases.

I would listen to the clients pouring their hearts out in desperation for help, and I would tell them to put it in Jesus' hand, and hold on to Him because He can do all but fail! Some of the other things that I would do for the nine caseworkers, included checking out or verifying address, dropped payments off to the furniture stores with vouchers for items needed for clients as soon as possible. These items included single bedding, dining table, lamps or something the doctor or medical staff recommended and the health insurance did not cover.

My son's mother had issues, like most of us do or should I say we all do. We are not perfect; only He is, Jesus. I chose not to be part of that confusion, but a father to my sons near or far! Every morning at 6 a.m. I would wake up to the Tom Joyner Morning Show; I listened out for Real Fathers, Real Men. I know now that every male could not fill the shoe that was about to be placed onto my feet, "Real Fathers Real Men."

A restraining order was filed against me through Family Court. I had no contact with my sons for about six months. One evening I was driving thru Back Maryland dropping a co-worker to her home. As I was making a loop to head home, I saw my two boys playing on a City playground in the back Maryland area. My oldest Wesley 3rd, recognized my 4X4 Jeep, he immediately screamed "Daddy, Daddy, Daddy!" His brother Christopher looked up and joined in with the screams for Daddy. They were running hard trying to get my attention; I viewed this incident from my rear view mirror - pulling off with tears streaming down my face, I told Jesus, Thanks for that unexpected crossing of our path, but to give me strength and provide care for their safety and well-being. The tears kept flowing as their physical images disappeared from my view. This was one of the lowest day of my life. Jesus had turned things around within months, because He naturally had my back and I am covered in His blood!

My daughter was a new born; I had bought a case of his and hers diapers for both children. Just days afterward, I got a phone call from the mother's friend telling me the children needed diapers.

I told her I just purchased both diapers a few days ago. Where are they? She informed me. I asked where the mother was, but she didn't know. I hadn't seen her since the Saturday I purchased diapers and had them dropped off to her by a cousin of mine! I was informed that they could use some over the counter cough medicine. I told her I was on my way. I was there in fifteen minutes; I decided to bring them back home with me. What little money I had I brought medicine. I stopped by my office and took the instamatic camera. I took a group shot, to show just the way they were abandoned. I cleaned and fed them and put them to bed in my room. It was about 10 pm, I got my "Basic Instructions Before Leaving Earth" (Bible) out and took my situation to Jesus. Didn't need a cell phone, I had my knees for a direct connection for His guidance. I called the Director at home the next morning to inform him of my situation and that I planned to go to family court; therefore, I needed a sick day, which he granted. I dropped the kids off to a babysitter, family friend's home. I returned the camera to the Welfare officer. I had taken a few pictures of the children, one for the courts, and two for me. I headed for family court, which was just down the street. I left my car parked in front of the office entrance of Tennessee and Arctic Avenues. The judge granted my temporarily custody after seeing the picture of the conditions in the way they were left. I enrolled my oldest son at Uptown Complex, my middle child at Head Start in the seven hundred block of Mediterranean Avenue, and my daughter back to the family friend, babysitter's home located right around the corner from where we lived. Their mother was still missing in action; much later down the road I was granted full custody; that made it permanent. I seldom believe, Jesus is not there when we need Him, but when He shows, He is right on time! Some males that I knew were fathers away from their children home front. Making ends meet, eating at Sister Jean's, a community soup kitchen or the mission, exchange value for some pocket change. My kids were enrolled in the Wic program that gave us formula, juices, cheese, and milk up to a certain age. A couple of people that worked down at the Goodwill store would hold on to some things for the children, knowing it would be deeply appreciated. I was working part time with a private security, watching the heavy equipment, used to tear down the establishments.

The children's mother was ordered to pay child support, (very little), but she still refused. Warrants were issued and a few law enforcement officers made it their business for her to take care of her business. She never visited when ordered to by the court, every other weekend, no overnight stay. I had no problem with her visiting. The children and I got back into the fold of going to church. The children were baptized and sang on the Rose Bud Youth Choir at Second Baptist Church. It was for youth ages five years old to twelve years of age.

I was involved with the security ministry. One day near the end of a special service, the smell of smoke was strong. I helped direct people out of the church. I had them to call in smell of smoke to 911!

Wires were burning located by A.C.F.D. in the wall it could have caused a major fire! But Jesus, nobody but Jesus we were under His protection, the umbrella of His love. There was so much love and support during that time at Second Baptist Church that kept me focused on the power of Jesus. After the passing of my mother, I had taken up time with the late Rev. I.S. Cole. Rev. Cole helped me to understand my mother stills walks with me and with Jesus. We redeveloped a strong relationship him as my shepherd for Christ, a long history from childhood to adulthood with connections at Second Baptist Church!

A few other churches had a role in my upbringing, maybe that's why I feel it's so important to take your children to church because you start that relationship with Christ, and build on a foundation that will help them in this world of life. Our newest pastor at S.B.C. that replaced another pastor who was selected after the death of Rev. I.S. Cole who passed eleven months after my mother. Jesus had brought me through that storm and helped me prepare for the next unexpected storm, that I did not know what was on the horizon. The pastor, his wife, and their children were so helpful with me and my children. My daughter would be picked up from Head-Start (school) to spend time over their home. I would pick her up after morning services at 11 a.m., it got so that I wouldn't have to pack things for her, because the pastor's family provided not only time into their home, but they would have things for her to wear to church. The first lady kept her hair looking nice, and showed her the love Jesus has from those around and for her.

I went to a Baptism Ceremony, afterward we spoke to the newest members of S.B.C.; I was sitting next to the Pastor, when I stood up to speak and I started telling about the history of the church.. Some forty-five years later I'm still here, praising Him. I wanted to let you know I belong to the Security Ministry, and also the Peanut Butter Ministry. The Pastor took a double look at me! I help all over! I looked toward him and said "No matter what ministry you claim, if you need my help contact me. You will have my support in helping the ministry in reaching its goal." It was well accepted over the years, Jesus granted me the opportunity without any recognition of my help in ministries doing the labor for the Lord. A coworker and a faithful member of S.B.C. helped keep me in tune with church activities and programs for the love of Christ, because He has done so much for me.

Switching gears, the "Tom Joyner Morning Show" was coming to the newly-opened Trump Taj Mahal Casino. It would be the first time in the Casino, with show time beginning at 6 p. m. with four hours live broadcast on the 96.1 FM Radio Station, WTTH! I knew people from the tri-state area would be in attendance, I made arrangements to have the children up and dressed to start their day. Of course they had to eat their breakfast. I planned to be home by 7:35 a.m. to get them to school and the babysitter, and to be on time to open doors for the clients needing assistance in my office of City Welfare.

The day of the T.J.M.S., I got up early about 4 a.m. I was dressed and out the door about twenty minutes later I was standing in line for T.J.M.S. about 4:55 a.m. There must have been six hundred people in front of me in line, six people across. Behind me the line was also six across and was wrapped to this long hallway! People were still coming in from the Boardwalk and the self-park garage. I had worn a shirt and tie and my Omega Psi Phi, Fraternity Jacket. They started seating at 5 a.m. that was when the line started to move slowly. When the group of people that I was standing with reached the entrance door to the theater big room, they were directing towards the back of the hall. I stepped out from the crowed and said pretty loud "Where's my class, where's my class?" and they looked up towards me. I broke from the crowd and walked over towards them. I made others think I was a teacher and that was my class sitting nearby; they were who I was looking for. I walked past their seating area right up front and came across a few members of Second Baptist Church., sitting up front fifteen yards from the stage! Tom Joyner was warming up the crowd, then walked up to his seat on the stage. He stop at the table where we were sitting, he spoke with the front end of the table, and went on to the stage. During the show Tom Joyner looked in our seating direction, and said, "Where's that table from Baltimore Maryland." The front stood up and we from S.B.C. joined the group as though we were all from Baltimore, everybody

106

at the table raised the level of excitement. Soon after, it was time for me to leave. As I was walking out, Bro. Tom Joyner and my path crossed. He recognized me among the many people in attendance; we gave each other the fraternity hand shake. I noticed, a local freelance photographer with his camera, I asked him to take a picture of the Que Dogs (Depend on God.) Someone yelled out because of the time it was taking for him to snap the picture and Brother Tom Joyner having to return to the stage to get back on the air radio waves. The camera has no films someone yelled, he snapped the picture the flash went off and we went our separate ways. As I stepped outside the door of the theater that seats approximately sixteen hundred people, it looked like about two hundred people in line trying to get in the first hour of the broadcast had passed. I did what I had to do for the children that morning.

I got to work at my normal time 8:15 a.m. and opened the doors at 8:30, fifteen minutes later. In the office, I had my radio tuned in to T.J.M.S. live from Taj Mahal Casino in Atlantic City! I was about to turned into a weekend warrior with my three young children.

Monday the first day back to work after going to the T.J.M.S. at the Taj, the local photographer "C.B." dropped off the photo of Tom Joyner and me,"I told you I had film in the camera", I hooked him up with some cash for the photo. I had enlarged several copies and I gave one copy to my breakfast place at Dave's Store, and hung the other in the waiting room where I worded it, my wall of fame. Pictures of my children doing different activities, church, soul circus, newspaper clipping of them, the Cowboys, Pete Hunter, certificates that the children were awarded, and the Omega Psi Phi with the dogs out and about, a lot of material about what kept me going and having Jesus. Real Fathers and Real Men, showed me encouragement for my soul. Again, jealousy sometimes raised its head, but I didn't have time. It was my wall of fame; it grew over the twelve years of being employed at City Welfare.

Reading the newspaper one morning, I came across an article in the paper that a Atlantic City Police officer committed suicide, and lived on top of a bar near Chelsea and Atlantic Avenue. This officer was one that went to the rehab. My partner had to tell what happened to the car they used, and how it got damaged. I cannot believe a red flag didn't pop up when the officer changed his address to a Tavern where he lived upstairs. This situation could have turned out much worst, some things are better kept about in the dark. The department made such an issue on after care of the officers that were sent away for substance abuse. It was demanded by the City at least three, twelve-step meetings a week. My question is, did they really care? Why no red flags popped up when this officer changed his address? Especially where he moved to! "And The Beat Goes On"!

Chapter Eleven

"Real Fathers, Real Men"

The children were getting bigger, and they needed room to grow. There was no place for single father that had custody of their children to live. There are all kinds of government programs and some private ones that helped aid females have stability with their family. The Mayor was walking through our department one day with Ms. Kitty. I asked him if he could direct me to getting an apartment so I can get out of cramped quarters at home. The Mayor looked at my wall frame, and he told me that he would get back with his Chief of Staff, Ms. Kitty. In about two weeks she would direct me as to what I should do. Two weeks had passed and she was still waiting on her source of information to contact her.

A special commission that was formed by the Federal Government was established, to research the effect of gaming in the United States, this included Atlantic City. I believe this study is done every ten years, by the Federal Commission and this was their second time coming to our City. I informed the Mayor I would pack my children into my Rodio 4X4, drive onto the beach wearing my city-issued uniform, in front of the Trump Taj, after calling every news station and media print to see how a city employee who has custody of his children and did not have adequate housing. So no matter what the report may give, a stain would be on it, because of the lack of housing. The Mayor asked me to wait, he would get back with me and he did the very next day.

About a week later, I went in to do my paperwork with the Atlantic City Housing Authority. I was granted an apartment at the Shore Park low rise. I was supposed to move in on August 1st, 1997. A friend of mine had drowned on the first beach in the Inlet after saving two children. The current took him out after he passed the children to some persons standing on the jetty. After the funeral had passed, I got it together to make the move to my roomy, new living condition. We moved into the so-called "Hostile Neighborhood." with having no authority or gun. This move was about my children staying together, being in each other's life, and them not being placed into foster homes throughout the state. I considered myself as a people person, a child of God, and a responsible father. I lived there for a total of eleven years, never having any problems with the neighbors, nor having police to be called over a dispute.

My boys were about to be picked on, but I nipped it in the bud real early. This young juvenile boy, I witnessed him put some dirt in my mail slot. I had just mopped the floors and was sitting on my porch, looking downward from my second floor, when he alone ran off my steps. I went to his apartment. He and his mother, walked across to my door. I showed them the mess that was created by his actions. His mother started sweeping it up. I told his mother it would not have been my child; and, at that time she swung the broom at him trying to take his head off. He took off running back to his apartment with his mom right on his heels, swinging my broom at him like she was Jackie Robinson! I reported it to the rent office the next day; a few days later a meeting was held with both parents agreeing to have no contact, staying away from each other.

Same family, different male child, again I were sitting on my balcony when I heard him say to my oldest son who was about ten years old, you'd better not tell. All kind of things were trying to enter my mind, in what he had told my son! I let him know that is my son, and he can talk with me about any and everything. He does not have to live in fear from anything or anybody. Therefore, I strongly suggest when you see mine, say something good to them or " keep a steppin."

Over the years this child witnessed how I took control by making my sons bring in grocery bags or packages, and taking my children out, or coming in spending time with them. He would help us bring packages in and I would offer drinks or some Barbeque if I grilled on the balcony. He started calling me, Mr. Wes! I had his friend clean the stairs, a spill that was made by accident, Once when we returned back home I witnessed a police officer step out of range with his authority with this young man. Surprisingly, he did everything the officer requested. I was hoping he wouldn't refuse and be arrested. He wasn't arrested and he was able to go on his way after being questioned,. I walked over to him and spoke with him, telling him what I witnessed was not fair to him. I stated "I can understand your being upset, that officer has a lot to learn and if he does not know what goes around, comes around, the cop better be ready for it to happen."

The Housing Authority promised on my lease, a clean safe protective environment in which to live for my children and me. We had closed circuit cameras at each entrance leading into the complex that could be seen in the entire courtyard, although it was said the cameras never functionally operated. The cameras were pointed up to the sky. I asked the rent office to just point cameras downward, having people thinking it's possible they do operate. That request fell on deaf ears. I was sitting at my dining room table one evening hearing a large number of different gun shots. It appeared to be a shootout in the complex across the street. Some were on bikes, while two cars had shots ringing out of it and a crowd of teenagers poured out into the streets. Police were notified and a description and direction of the fight was given. No arrest was ever made to this incident.

The view I had from my dining room area window gave me a lot of vision. The bottom line is I stayed focused on Jesus Christ. Not having the talent of doing my daughter's hair, I paid for different women to wash and style her hair, when needed.

One evening, I got a call from a friend who was coming into town from Mays landing, about a half hour ride on the bus. She stated, I could pick her up from the bus station, and she would come over fix my daughter' hair. I said, "Okay, call me when you get in town." She did call, and I picked her up from the bus station, and we headed for my home. We were stopped at the corner one block from my apartment at a red light. It was lightly raining, across from us was a motorcycle coming toward the red light. The light turned green for both of us heading in the opposite direction. I chose to let him pass through the intersection before I pulled off. As he drove by to my left side we both looked at each other. He made a U-Turn; I told the young lady get ready we are going to be stopped. I had pulled over right below my apartment window, several police vehicles came as his backup. I didn't have my license on me, but mistakenly, I left them in my uniform shirt pocket. I asked if my passenger could go get them out my house for me. The officer said "no!". About six minutes passed by, I had given him my name, address, date of birth, and I told him I was en route to have my daughter's hair done. By this time my children were looking out the window, seeing me standing at the rear of my car in the rain! Now, it has started picking up in raindrops.

Eventually my passenger was allowed to retrieve my license. When she passed it to me, I passed it to the officer. He gave them right back to me, and he had already ran my name, only to find no warrants, a good driving record, and no points cleared. I was tied up for about twenty-two minutes. The officer said, I was stopped because of my broken tail light. It was not noticeable unless you were standing right up on it. It was a hairline crack on the lens. I would have had more respected for that officer if he had stated, because of the criminal activity in the area and we are checking everybody out, and saying sorry for the inconvenience. I have no problem with that. My children were wondering why I was standing in the rain. I was soaked and I was sent on my way. I locked my car doors and walked into my apartment knowing what that was really about!

About three weeks later, after my motor vehicle stop, right under my window, from our apartment dining area, I was cleaning up after serving dinner. I had to wash dishes, put the food away and what little leftovers it may have been, swept the floor and took the trash out. All of a sudden I heard some type of argument right outside my window. I called 911 to report some kind of unknown trouble in the nine hundred block of Mediterranean Avenue. A male was yelling at the top of his voice, which got my attention three levels up. The male was standing in the street ordering the driver to put her window down. I noticed a gray minivan parked right behind it with the motor running. The minivan had P.A.L. of Atlantic City printed on the side. I opened my window, lifting the screen. Hanging my head out the window yelling down is everything all right. The male signaled as if motioning things were ok. I noticed it was a female driver that was being yelled at. It was a motor vehicle stop, I called 911 back to let them know to disregard the police cars because the officer had let the driver go. She had pulled off in her vehicle. This officer did not follow police procedure on or off duty; when making a motor vehicle stop, you must call it in, for the safety of the public, driver, and the police stopping the vehicle. It is documented and recorded. If you don't have radios, get the car tag plates. Use your cell phone if it's that important, or use a public pay phone. If something would happen to the officer making the stop (God forbid), an all-out war would have been waged with police officers against males in the hood. Reasons for this kind of developed information would lead to the arrest of the injured if not slain cop attacker. Because of this officer's negligence, not calling in his motor vehicle stop. Thank you Jesus, no one got hurt. Looking through my windows at the streets, below I continue to pray for all who foot prints were outside my window. This is just some of the problems I had to deal with in my Hood!

Because of the poor conditions, apartments becoming vacant, some not clean when tenants moved out. Boarded up, apartments resulted in infestations. Extermination on its monthly schedule only to those apartments occupied. Keeping in mind, possible arson from, the Atlantic City.. Housing Authority protection was there!

Drug activity was off the hook, but again I got the respect when I was home, they would move off my stairs. I was the only occupied apartment in my cove, out of four apartment doors in a cove.

The office management did not take any action whatsoever; she was concerned that nothing happened to her new car. She told me that the last car she had was keyed or scratched by a young female that she had problems with. She said to me she could not prove it was her, so she does nothing, to keep her car scratch free. But when you claim to be washed in his blood, why would you fear evil? Eleven years, I lived in public housing, the mismanagement, the conditions causing health and stress on my children and me. I decided to move my family out! I left voluntary moving back into Bungalow Park in which we originated from. I'm in possession of documents from the housing authority claiming just that. Voluntarily, I'm on the "Hope Six" list. This entitles families to new housing! I'm entitled to have the same benefit as if I was paying rent to the authority on monthly bases. The Housing Authority still has its problems from the com-missioners who sat on the board, down to its tenants. I felt this is just a test - all that has happen to me!

A few years before I chose to voluntarily move out of Shore Park, a second African American male - a Democrat - was voted in as the Mayor of Atlantic City. He, too, is a member of Omega Psi Phi Fraternity, Inc.; and one of my line Brothers. It was twelve of us that pledged into Omega; yes, a picture of our line was placed on my office "Wall Of Fame".

I was in a store playing the "Omega" Lottery. The Mayor's brother in-law also a Que, a line Brother of ours said to me "Frat likes how you have been taking care of your children, being a single parent." Do not worry Wes, you will be hearing from him. Your position will be upgraded, that will increase your salary; therefore, you will be able to take better care of your family needs. I'm still playing the Omega Jackpot game. We laughed, played and went our separate ways. Not surprisingly, I did not get my promotion until about the last sixteen months before the Mayor lost his second bid to stay in as Mayor for another four year term. I always depended on Jesus, and his Father, for my blessings, not man!

I moved into the position of Welfare Investigator, I passed the written exam and had Civil Service Protection. Because of the politics in Atlantic City, the "dog and pony" show, I kept my focus on what I had to do for my children - keeping them together, having a roof over their heads and food in the refrigerator. I try never to be judgmental toward any person, sex, race, religion or wealth. That's one hard pill for me to swallow when you take aim at my children, I pray not to ever become a hater, filled with jealously, but by reading this book, being one of His children, "they should have known to leave me alone"! Maybe it may become clearer to its reader. I started to realize there will always be haters; these are some people that express they know the working of Jesus and his Father God. They think they can go right to God, without Jesus. I know that's wrong; some of these folks attend church on a regular basis and may even belong to a ministry function in the church, but deeply planted in their soul or heart is jealously. They may talk, the talk, but differently do not walk the walk. Some may even say they are praying for you but in reality, make your own connection with Christ. He will see you through, Jesus can do all, but the only thing He can't do, is fail!

I was employed with City Welfare, a total of about twelve years. My last position was Welfare Investigator. I held it for 16 months, before it was phased out. The Atlantic County Welfare took over the City function of welfare. Because of this faze out of City Welfare, I believe another step was being taken to eventually eliminate the lower economical residents of Atlantic City. I, being one of the many who came through the doors of City Welfare for much needed assistance, truly had pros and cons of City Welfare being shut down.

Some of the City Welfare employees retired, transferred to the county to continue social services or placed in other city departments. Even one relocated to the South. One thing for sure, if you can survive in New Jersey for any period of time, you can live anywhere beyond its boarder as long as you have Christ. That makes it more victorious.

Everyone had made their move by March of 2006. A state worker assigned from Trenton, the Director of Public Assistance and I loaded up some cases that were still active, carted them over to the County building across the courtyard from City Hall. This process continued over a two month period. The program hat the City offered for individuals for assistance did a great job, in the community. Clients reported every month to their caseworkers to continue benefits. We got to know clients seeing them around during our daily life activities. I witnessed other communities having their police dropping off people in our City in need of help, most of the time needing a one way ticket to get back home. There were guidelines for such assistance set by the State. Each municipality, township or borough was to take the responsibility to assist those in their jurisdiction. Instead some agencies had them report to the Rescue Mission or City Welfare. That made it Atlantic City's responsibility to get the person and at times children with them back home, a one way ticket, gas and toll money for those with vehicle.

I was told by one of my union white collar officials, that they didn't want to give me another position. She demanded it was the proper thing to do, because "I was a single, responsible parent in the household and my children deserve it!" A decision was made that I will be reporting to the Police Athletic League, as a Security Guard. The union official told me to watch my back because they don't want you over there and the first thing they can hang something on, you will be done. I stand with Jesus, we all know the saying, "Not a weapon formed against me will prosper." She prayed for my continue blessing and to keep my faith. I notified the Atlantic County Prosecutor Office to let them know how I could be contacted if needed pending on a few cases that were being reviewed by a Grand Jury. I gave them my new position and a phone number on where to reach me!

Chapter Twelve

"Have Mercy On Them!"

Although Welfare was closed, in March of 2008, I helped with the cases that had to be loaded onto a push cart and transported across the way to the County Building. June 2, 2006 was my first day to report as a Security Guard for the PAL Center. I reported to a church member, who was head of recreation for youths to provide some activity for school age children. She directed me to speak with the police officer that headed the PAL Center. He had no rank in the Police Department, but politically was given that position. This police officer told me I had seniority over the other two security officers with regard to hours worked and lunch break! One of the guards that had been working for some time was bent out of shape because he was losing his choice of hours to work, and lunch break, one half hour. Although his time was never watched when he would be missing, nothing was ever said, about him missing in action.

I was given keys to the Center, on the third day of reporting for work. One key was for the main front entrance of the PAL Center, and the second key was for the security office, where one would have a view of the outer area. Three out of six security cameras were operational throughout the center. The third was for the staff restrooms. The security officer that was bumped who worked day-shift, did not work seven hours daily as I. He only had to work five days. (Monday thru Friday).

The director of the PAL Center didn't want both security guards reporting to work at the same time because the complex would normally be empty during early morning hours, except the Golden Circle that consists of senior citizens using the gym. Persons fifty and above (age) would meet for early morning activities. I let him work his hours for about three weeks until my children ended their school year at Oceanside Charter School, located just blocks away. I was given a half hour lunch break from 12:30 p.m. until 1 p.m. I felt, that everything I did was under watch, as though a time watch was used. There was nowhere I could physically go to get lunch for takeout under a half hour. Even if I called it in for pickup, finding a parking space, line at the cash register, not to mention people wanting to see how you are doing, since the changes at City Hall. It would take much longer than a half hour, I decided not to leave the Center for lunch. Instead, I would sometime bring something to eat with me, or I would call my dad, or a few of my friends that work in patrol, on Alpha Platoon. They made sure I had something to eat because I was a diabetic. It was not a problem for me to have lunch this way. But as you can guess, others that were in the click or the anti-Langford group, that worked at the PAL Center did what they wanted to do, one and a half hour lunch, early out. (leaving work early before their schedule ended) My connection with Langford was when we pledged into Omega Psi Phi Inc.; Upsilon Alpha Chapter. I had my pride in him being Mayor, but I had more focus in doing the right thing for Jesus, my children for which I was responsible. I was never into treating a person differently because of their political belief. There were some of "those" that made the policy at PAL and treated me horribly, but being a man of Christ, belonging to Fraternity, you must have a high level of tolerance and hold on to your faith. I was in the protection of my Savior, Jesus Christ!

Between the several times of being called into the "Executive Director" office of the PAL Complex for conflicts that I had no control of, the keys were taken from me by the patrolman.

This is the same person who made a motor vehicle stop right outside my window, the officer that didn't follow police procedure in making the motor vehicle stop.

On rainy, cold or windy days, I had to wait until someone from maintenance, opened the door for me to enter the building. They would normally be working on the first level at the time. I would arrive for work at 8:15 a.m., but numerous times, I would have to walk up the ramp to the third level in the rear of the PAL Center to gain entry because maintenance would be working at that level in the area, sweeping or mopping. I would say nothing about it and did my job regardless without having or showing an attitude. I had hung pictures of my children and some Fraternity activities on the wall. This is something that was natural for many of the working people, would do. No matter how a stressful situation occur dealing in my duties or position I held, it would remind me by looking at these pictures, stress has no effect on my achievements, it was Jesus, helping me keep my balance.

The young co-worker continued to be very bitter towards me because he was forced to switch his hours at work. Again, I tried to work with him by not taking my requested hours of work on start day but rather three weeks after being assigned to the PAL Center. This person took my pictures down that I had on the wall.

In a backpack, he carried to work Hip-Hop magazines and D.V.D. movies with things that exposed nudity, foul language, and things that made me feel uncomfortable. He and some of his buddies would entertain themselves on the job with these items! Because, young children and seniors not to mention, were sometimes in this area, where he did his entertaining. His friends would come into the office to watch and read or should I say look at the pictures in the magazines. I felt so uncomfortable that I started staying out of this office.

I stationed myself behind the front desk across from the Receptionist, but it was one of the two desks the police officer's secretary used. I wasn't allowed to sit behind it at all. This woman, I kept my distance from her because of her unprofessional attitude. She's not stupid, she realized who to pull it on and who not to.

A woman came in there one day, and threatened to turn her every way but loose on how she had spoken to her child! With the assistance of others who overheard the disruption; we were able to separate them and walk the child's mother out of the center. She got control of herself and went on her way. I never had a complaint about my attitude, language or disrespect towards any person, youth, senior citizens, or visitors that came into the PAL Center for whatever their purpose. Because of the tension, with the click and being a mature, educated, single parent, I was treated as though I was the new kid on the chopping block. Yes, there was a person before I started at PAL, which was mistreated and abused by the police officer that headed PAL Yes, that same officer, lost the hearing/charges he had filed against her, costing the city a lawsuit for damages. Yes, she got her job reinstated, cash settlement put back to work at another job location, away from those misfits, who don't know how to be a professional, but instead, a circus with clowns!

Turning back to the summer of '04, when my line brother who was the second Black elected as the Mayor of Atlantic City, had a summer job program for residential children, that met certain requirements such as grades, attendance, not being a disciplinary problem to the school or community. I would suppose based on family need. It consisted of five days a week, for six weeks, about six and half hours daily. Many children would apply but only those who successfully complete this job orientation which was held at the PAL Center would be considered for employment!

My oldest son received a position to work for the City as a youth summer participant Wesley, was six foot three inches, weighing about two hundred and twenty five pounds. He was much taller and heavier than I. He was a big, healthy, strong very kindhearted, young teenager! He was given a position to help transport on City owned buses that provided transportation for its seniors to go food shopping. Atlantic City didn't have a Supermarket on the island; therefore, daily they would take the seniors to food shopping. They had three youths that helped the seniors load and unload their groceries from the bus.

My son was paid minimum wages with payday every two weeks. Surprising to me, he was making tips from those who knew him and some of them were from church. My son was an incoming freshman at Atlantic City High School. The tips he made came in as another blessing, because he could buy things he needed for school. It helped with the budget we were on. The next summer of '06, I had transferred to the PAL Center. The job or position was not available with the City. I spoke to brother "L" and he told me not to worry, and that my son would get a job for the summer of '06. About three days later our paths crossed on the streets, when he pulled or should I say Ray, his assigned Police Officer, pulled along-side of me, waiting at a traffic light. He informed me that I should call the A.C. Surf and ask for the general manager, and that he was expecting my call.

The Baseball Stadium is located several blocks passed the Peter Egnor/Albany Avenue Bridge. My son started working with special events held Saturday and Sunday way before regular baseball season started in June. I believe my son was very happy, working and I thank, Jesus again for bringing joy into my heart, for his many countless times that He has given us!

Meanwhile back at P.A.L, again I was starting to feel very uncomfortable, (not because of my diabetes) one morning, I was drinking some coffee and eating an egg sandwich, while reading the Press (a local newspaper). I was listening to a local talk show on the radio. Former Mayor "Langford" was a guest on the show and he was attempting to explain something that occurred when he was the sitting Mayor. Out of nowhere, the police officer of PAL. "the cop," or H.N.I.C. unnoticed to me, was standing in the security office, and started yelling, "he's a damn liar!" I was shocked, because the radio was not loud. I was into reading the paper, and getting some much needed nutrition into my body. Again, I've seen the side of a mad, man with a gun. At that point, I began my morning upstairs on the second level in the gym basically away from him. Some people would come in to use the gym to walk the floor to get exercise. One councilman seemed to start his day off by shooting basketball with himself between calls on his cell phone.

There is a supervisor that has numerous issues, which will be revealed in just a matter of time. Again, no one is perfect, but when you act as if you are sheep, but deep beneath is that wolf, it's just a matter of time for it to be exposed to the light. I can only pray for you and ask for Jesus to have mercy on you! Life is a full circle, what goes around, comes around! I'm not going to say any more, let's keep it moving!

This one brother whose starting time was twelve noon for about five hours, Monday thru Friday graduated in the Class of 1975 Atlantic City High School with me. We would sit upstairs and exchange stories about our past, present or future. Some days he had his ups or his downs. Sometimes I would get permission to go pickup his lunch or I give him a ride home, because of his illness. He was a good person; he later passed shortly after I received my departmental charges that caused me my livelihood, to care for my family.

My dad went up to New York on a five day trip in which he drove. He left Saturday and returned the following Wednesday morning on April 3rd, 2007. That Monday April 1st, 2007, and I dropped my children at Oceanside Charter School at 7:55 a.m., I stopped to pick-up my lunch at a nearby Deli. I reported to work thereafter, it was approximately 8:15 a.m. I entered the P.A.L. complex using the rear second level ramp, I went downstairs to sign in, before doing my security check. It was about 8:50 a.m. when my co-worker showed up using his key entering the complex. He spotted me in the security office. He wanted to know why I was at work, because my report time was 9 a.m. I totally ignored his request, informing him why I was at work so early. I was out from my home, doing what I had to do, I signed in the time I arrived. He was given new hours to work and to see me there at work he thought I was pulling seniority on him. I had no idea of this change, at that time. On the same day, April 1st Monday in the afternoon, I had come out of the staff restroom when I saw my coworker talking with this young adult male, dressed in dark clothing wearing a hoodie. The male quickly exited the P.A.L complex as I was walking towards them. At the front entrance, at that time a police officer, a friend of mine came into the P.A.L. He informed me, what had just happen up on the other corner at Kentucky and Mediterranean Avenue, a shooting!

The shooting suspect a black male, wearing dark clothing with a hoodie, was seen running up towards the P.A.L complex. I strongly believe that was the male trying to enter the complex, who was talking to my co-worker. The police officer attempted to get some information from him, but he stated he didn't see anything or anybody. The surveillance cameras didn't work, and we didn't have a taped recording of the suspect talking with security. When my friend left to continue the search for the suspect, some co-workers asked me, "was I crazy!" "You don't involve me with the police, I got to go home, I live in this hood and I'm not getting involved!" I got heated and told them, "These children, seniors, and your co-workers' safety is our responsibility. You don't want the word on the street to be that the P.A.L is a safe haven to hide if you're involved in criminal activity from the police. The Staff won't say anything if they see, that you are bringing trouble inside these walls. You're supposed to have the community's well-being at hand, working here! "This

Circus" really is not funny but sad for the people that depend, and enjoy the facility.

Chapter Thirteen

"They Should Have Known
To Leave Me Alone!"

O n Tuesday, the next day of reporting for work at 8:20 a.m., I called a computer instructor that worked for the Atlantic City Housing Authority. His office was located just around the corner from the PAL Center, and it was in the two hundred block, North Kentucky Avenue, in the first villages of Stanley Holmes. I needed him to figure out why our home computer could not complete its task. The children needed it to complete their school projects. "John" instructed me to call him back; I would pick him up to go home on his break between 12 noon and 1 p.m. that day. I told him I would call back to confirm just a few hours later.

After hanging up the phone, I went over to the executive director's office door (H.N.I.C.); he was sitting behind his desk eating some goods from Dunkin Donut and was reading the local newspaper. I knocked on his door saying good morning and I explained what I needed to do; I have not taken lunch breaks, leaving the complex. Also, I had reported early the past couple of days although my start time was 9 a.m. The officer stated I could go, but to sign out before I left. I thanked him and left his office. I informed my co-worker of my intentions for him to maintain the command post, doing his hip-hop thing video, and magazines thing in the security booth when I left!

I called John back to see if we still were going to connect to go to check out the computer. He said, "Wesley something may come up" I was waiting, but come around now; I will try to get it done for you. It was now, 1:15 p.m., which was the time I signed out; I couldn't locate my co-worker because he wasn't where he was assigned to be. I walked over to the receptionist's desk and informed her as to what the director said to me. She said, "Sign out, things are slow I'll let your co-worker know when he pops up." I left the PAL Center at 1:15 p.m., two minutes later right around the corner, I blew my horn and out came John saying, "Wesley we can't do it now." What I was waiting for, I must start it to have completed by today and take it up to the administration office. I said "Okay, but I know how to reach you", I put my minivan into reverse used the side street that lead me back to the PAL Center. I had signed back in at 1:35 p.m. A total twenty minutes I had left the center, signing back in, the receptionist stated things were still quiet. I thanked her and said it will always be a tomorrow, and boy was I right.

The same day, later in the afternoon before I went home the time was about 3:15 p.m., I was talking with the Health and Human

Services Supervisor, and the receptionist. One of the other supervisors with PAL which is under Public Safety budget or department, interrupted our conversation and stated he had a write-up for me to sign. I politely said to him, "Write up for what? What did I do?" He began reading it to me. When he finished reading it he attempted to have me sign his write-up! I refused for two reasons and I told him "One, it's not the truth, and two, I didn't have my glassed in order to read it for myself." He stated I left the P.A.L center not having authorization from the time of, 1:45 p.m. until 2:53 p.m. because he was looking for me and I could not be found. I was doing my job and I was back before you started your witch hunt toward me. I then continued my conversation with the two ladies.

Time passed it was time to get my things and sign out. On my way out, the click was sitting in the security office and some were looking at that hip-hop stuff in the magazine. Others, a D.V.D. filled with violence, nudity and strong language but this was their normal on a daily basis. I shook my head in disbelief, looking at the gathering of the misfit individuals that worked around youth and those seniors. Jesus knows who they are and in His time He will deal with them; I hope he gives them mercy on their actions around those to serve.

The next day, April 3rd, 2007, I arrived at work at 8:25 a.m. I pulled up in my minivan and attempted to park behind the PAL vehicle, which the "H.N.I.C." was driving. He could have pulled up some to allow me to park behind him. He was in a conversation with a male that known to me that frequent his office at PAL. I waited about eight minutes, but the H.N.I.C. didn't move his vehicle upward.

A car that was parked on the same side of the street had pulled out of its parking space and I drove around the P.A.L vehicle and parked my vehicle. I said "good morning" with the motion of my hand at both men sitting in the PAL vehicle. There was no response. I continued on my way into the center thinking the conversation between them must be deep because both seemed to be looking in my direction. After signing in, I did my security check around the perimeter and different three levels of the complex. When I finished, I went up to the second level and read the paper, had some coffee and watched a few people use the gym for their morning activity.

About 10:30, I was called downstairs to the security office by my co- security officer. He wanted me to stay in the office because he had something to do, and would be leaving the PAL Center. I'm a team player as mentioned before. He informed me that the mother (of the supervisor for PAL), had the key to the exercise equipment located on the third floor, those were the only keys out. I said Ok. I finished reading the newspaper in the security command office. About forty-five minutes later, the phone rang, and I answered; it was the mother calling and wanting to speak with her son. I informed her he was not in at this time; his police PAL van was not parked out front. I remember seeing her son and my co-worker take off in the van. She then asked me to have him call her at home. I said "Will do". I asked her did she forget to return the keys that were given to her for the equipment upstairs. She told me no, in a nasty loud voice and hung up the phone in my ear. At that time, I didn't understand why she came out like that at me.

About twenty minutes later, both so-called men returned, my co-worker had the keys and put them in their proper place in the file cabinet. P.A.L. Supervisor "4-12". was informed his mother had called and wanted him to return the call. They were both in possession of some kind of fast-food and a soft drink, please don't read between their lines! I went back upstairs at this time. Howard was on his post outside his boss's office door. We talked and he indicated to me that I was being watched by his boss "4-12."! I then got up and went back downstairs to heat up some soup that I wanted to eat. The "female click" was all sitting at a table eating some K.F.C. with some soft drinks. I spoke and opened the can of soup that I wanted, and placed it in the microwave. This female public works employee (maintenance) spoke to me as though I was a child or maybe her husband in a hostile manner, to clean up my mess! (which I had made none at that point). I told her "You got your people mixed up if I spoke to you like that, you'd be telling your husband how you were disrespected. This is not the time or place to have your feelings smashed." She got up and left the kitchen.

Moments later, the police officer came into the kitchen wearing his shoulder hostler over top of his jogging suit. He asked me to go into his office; I took my soup out of the microwave and covered it up with a napkin, and proceeded into his office. Thank God, through the way of Jesus, I left his office door open as I entered it.

He asked me, what happened with a confrontation that I had the day before. Confrontation? I guess I looked puzzled because I was drawing a blank facial expression; he said "Between you and coach." I told my version, I guess it was not good enough for him to accept, but it was the truth. When Supervisor "4-12"., read it to me, not being the truth, I refused to sign it, then he said, "Why were you going to get a gun and come to PAL and shoot the center up?" Then I asked several times to reveal who told him that, and he refused to answer. This conversation between us is over and I am going home (sick)! I got up from my seat, excused myself went directly to the kitchen wrapped my lunch then walked over to get my coat and bookbag to put my lunch in and then over to the receptionist's desk to sign out. One of the Recreation Secretaries came walking out from the back; it seemed she may have been in the restroom because she was wiping her hands dry with paper towels. I asked her to put me out, going home sick at 12:43 p.m., and she said "okay Wesley!" As I opened the door to exit, two Atlantic City Police Officers in uniform were entering the building. I stepped to the side to allow them entry saying hello and went on to my parked vehicle across the street. After making a three point turn and stopping at a red light waiting for the green light to proceed, a second police unit pulled facing the opposite direction of traffic, the cop jumped out and ran into the building. I said to myself, "Don't tell me this clown, (H.N.I.C.) called the police on me." The traffic light changed to "green", and I drove straight home. I was so glad, I never shut his office door and Jesus continued to keep me under his protection of the madness that's implanted in that P.A.L. Center.

My father had returned from his five-day trip to New York. He had brought back a castle box 32 White Castle Burgers for the children and me. I began heating everything up again for lunch, and I told my father what had happened at work. It seemed to have upset him very much! I walked out the kitchen, giving him time to vent; frustration set in, dad was truly upset. I entered the living room, looking out the Bay window. The microwave buzz sounded letting me know my lunch was ready to eat. I turned to walk away from looking out the window then I noticed the Swat Team along with other uniformed police officers gathering at the corner from my house, Connecticut and Caspian Avenue. I then walked back to the kitchen where my dad was standing, and I told him, what I just saw and I believed the Swat Team or officers gathering were coming to get me. At that time my father went to the front door to look outside.

A captain of police that join the force the same time I did asked my father was I home. At that time, I walked out the house. Stated to the Captain, all these officers were disrespectful and not needed. My dad is a retired police officer and that is what it's all about, making it to retirement. Also my dad collects a pension. As of April 1st, 2007, it was close to twenty-three years for him receiving his pension. I wouldn't disrespect my father, my children or myself. I invited the

Captain to choose any police officer that was standing out front with him to come into my dad's home and the remaining fifteen (15) officers send back into service clearing out the six hundred block Caspian Avenue.

The meeting between us turned out positive. It turns from criminal/police conversation to friends helping friends. I was never arrested by P.A.L. cop, the unknown police officers, who responded to the PAL Center when I was exiting from PAL, or any one of the S.W.A.T response team that came to my home. There was never a complaint lodged against me by youth, or senior citizen who used the center!

There seemed to be no policy to follow for H.N.I.C, when information was received of what I allegedly said. He should have brought it to the attention of his supervisors and I could have been brought in for questioning, like I stated, " I never said it." I don't allow my children to play with water guns, video games, and anything that is violent that uses a gun or gun-shaped figure. But watching those DVD's, listening to that gangster rap, your mind gets weak and you think you have no one you will have to answer too! If he had done things professionally, I would still have my job. But instead he is helping Jesus plan to come to fruition!

I want my readers to know, there was some remunerable moments at P.A.L. that I was glad to have experienced there!

John D. King, Ph.D., held a weekly program that consisted of juvenile offenders that had been found guilty by the courts. If they were accepted by Dr. King and complete this program it would be a great situation for the juvenile and his family. There would be no incarceration time for the offense committed, but they had to undertake the expectation that they would place on you by Dr. John King. This was no Joke! For some, it was easier to serve the time! If Dr. King informs the courts you violated a requirement, your start date being incarcerated starts from day one, no matter how much time you put in the program! Those involved included Youth from around the county, male and female, from single parent homes, some with no father in their life, being around or grandparents raising a child or children. Dr. John King and I would talk about the changing time of the inner city youth. Drugs, guns, the disrespect for human life was taking its shape across America and on the sand of our shore!

Other than the juvenile offenders, some mothers of those juveniles, men just being released from incarceration, some on probation would be in attendance! They would share with the group how easy it is to get yourself caught in the system and how hard it is to stay out of it, but it can be done. It's up to you to make the right choices in life, having free will. At one of the weekly meetings, Dr. John King had to address a couple of the male juveniles. One male was told to go in the men's room, pull his pants up, and tuck his shirt inside his pants! The other was told to cut off the cell phone and sit up in his class. He further stated that all he had to do was call the county and the juvenile would start from day one. Remember you don't know when you will see me, or hear from me by phone. "Learn to keep it together, not for me, but most importantly yourselves" stated Dr. John King!

My oldest son, unexpectedly showed up during a weekly meeting. I would get off at 4:30 p.m., but I would leave twenty minutes later at the end of the meeting. My oldest son came in one week and had a seat during my five-week participation. I spoke that day about how hard it was being a single male parent! But I knew everything was going to be alright because I had someone who stands high and looks low (Jesus!) At that time my son, who was six foot, three inches tall, about two hundred and thirty-five pounds, graduating from the eighth grade, stood up! This meeting serves a two-fold purpose. One, to show the class that my son has Jesus and I, keeping it moving, no problems in or out of school with any kind of authority. Second, to show my son to stay focused, because the system wants you to not achieve high school; therefore you are certain to become of not having your freedom eventually. It worked for my son because he did graduate from high school never getting out of line with me! (all praises to my Savior)

The other remunerable moment was meeting and talking with a professional law-enforcement police officer! I had heard about him, and read about some of the arrests he had made in the press. But when he won the election to become the union leader for the P.B.A., Local #24, I was keyed in reading the paper. Yes, Officer David Davidson, Jr. President of P.B.A. Local #24, had a lot on his plate to handle Police Officers basic issues. I have seen him at Second

Baptist Church at 11 a.m. services on Sunday a number of times. He is someone who always smiles when greeting you! He has an ear for listening in what is being said. He once surprised me by sending a gift that was greatly appreciated by my children and me, just before Christmas one year! He also included a maroon sweatshirt, with A.C.P.D. printed on it. It was from the Local #24.

He had a son that was on the force, like father, like son! Oh what a feeling!(GREAT) During these rough, economical times across the country, people were losing their jobs and careers. The public safety had laid off police and fire personnel. They were out of work for about a year. It was just a test because most were rehired even my buddy's son! I met him, Phil, while he was working extra duty at the corner of M.L.K. and Pacific Avenues. We had a great conversation about things. I had let a few #2 Jitneys pass me by while talking to him; it was a pleasure to have met him.

Chapter Fourteen

"You Thought You Had Yours, But I Got Mine!"

The next day April 1st, 2007, I called out from work sick. I had enough of the mishaps, foul treatment and that cotton farm attitude most employees had for H.N.I.C. I put it to prayer. I started feeling much better as the day progressed. "I am the master of my faith and the Captain of my soul", and I will sail on, no matter what the storm displays. Later that morning, I received a letter from the Director of the City Office of Human Resources. I was being suspended immediately without pay, effectively today, April 4th, 2007. The charges filed against me were incompetency, inefficiency, or failure to perform duties, insubordination conduct unbecoming a public employee; also, two other sufficient causes, violation of Section X of the City of Atlantic City Employee Personal and Procedures Manual, Section X, 2, 5, and 9. "The City of Atlantic City is hereby suspending you immediately; the City has determined that you are unfit for duty or a hazard to any person, if permitted to remain on the job, or that an immediately suspension is necessary to maintain safety, health, order or effective direction of public services.

I repeated "Jesus has my back" and I smiled up to him. This date April 4th, 2007, was my 13th year anniversary working for the City; they tried to kick me to the curb or throw me up under the bus. They didn't realize who my spiritual father was. Not only it being my anniversary of being hired, it was the day Martin Luther King was assassinated by a person with a gun.

On April 5th, or around that date, a federal agent was killed in the State of New Jersey, in Northern Jersey on a stake out of some bank robbers. I believe it was the first time an agent was killed in the line of duty in over ten years. He was accidentally shot and killed by a fellow agent. The F.B.I. stated they would be there on any needs the family may endure. In other words, they will stand by and support his wife and daughters; I knew who has been supporting me.

On the fourth day of my suspension, April 8th, 2007, a confused college student out in the Midwest, went on a shooting rampage on a college campus. He killed several people and caused harm to many. I'm only human and I'm not perfect, or do I act as though I am. The City tried to put a brush in my hand and make me think I was this violent, self-centered, non-responsible individual that would cause harm to others or myself in such a destructive manner.

Not so far from that date, at a shopping mall, in the Midwest, again in this country, a male individual shot and killed some person there. His last name was the same as mine. Yes, this wasn't any food for my thought, my plate had more than enough on it. I had to keep remembering who was in charge, not to worry, Jesus had my back!

During this time while being placed on suspension with the City, my supervisor who was one of the persons I was talking with when Supervisor 4-12, who pretends to be what he is not, stopped by and confronted me about signing that fictitious write-up. This supervisor also a confidential aid to the, then, Mayor Levy came over to my home at my request. The supervisor spoke with my dad and me. She stated to my dad she was shocked, how I let it roll off my back. I didn't get upset, I didn't raise my voice or even get disrespectful, I was totally professional!

I now had to wait on May 3rd, 2007, at 1 p.m. to have my hearing in this matter. My defense team, union white collar professional association, its lawyer, and the head man, Jesus Christ, took the hearing by storm!

The City took a potato (me) and added its own ingredients, with no evidence to make potato salad, and I was not eating it, not even a teaspoon of it. I won the hearing, but now the City demanded I see a psychiatrist. They informed me, I will be contacted on "whom they will choose" for me to see, to be revaluated, I did not, worry - my focus got even stronger to my spiritual father, and He does all but fail!

On May 26th, I was notified by the division of unemployment insurance based upon the facts obtained and in accordance with the New Jersey unemployment compensation law, I am eligible for benefits from 5-6-07, that date I applied for unemployment. "You were suspended without pay on 4-4-07. You stated your employer alleged you made a terrorist threat. There is no evidence to support this allegation. I was suspended for actions that do not constitute a willful and deliberate disregard of the standards of behavior your employer had a right to expect. Therefore, my suspension was not for misconduct with the work. You are eligible for benefits signed the director of the Division of Unemployment of the State of New Jersey."

The administration had set an appointment for me to have an office visit with their doctor for a psychiatric evaluation in Egg Harbor Township, New Jersey on May 18th, 2007. I wanted my job back, but allow me to be transferred out of that P.A.L mess! That's just what it was a "Mess" stinking. . .sooner or later. . .it will be flush. . .waste down the toilet. . .I have washed my hands. . .I'm finished!

I knew and felt comfortable that no weapon formed against me will ever prosper! I made confirmation of the appointment date.

That day, I showed up fifteen minutes before my scheduled appointment time, and prayed for His continuing protection. The doctor emerged from an outer office, walked over to where I was sitting, and asked me who I was. I told him my name. He asked me to follow him; we went to his office where he conducted my evaluation. I must mention, I had eye laser conducted on both my eyes that morning, and two hours later I met with the psychiatrist.

. He asked questions concerning my childhood memories of my parents, my sister, myself and growing up in Atlantic City. One hour later, according to his buzzer, he told me time was up! I asked him, are you going to ask me why I want my job! He said, "Business with you is over." I stood up from my chair position across from his desk. I extended my hand to shake with his. He looked over his glasses at me and said, "Trigger get out of here now!" Having nothing to say, I remembered who had my back. I went outside of his office; my ride had made a dash knowing he had to return shortly to drive me home.

As I was waiting, the doctor emerged from the office carrying his coat, briefcase, and his hat on his head. I spoke by saying have a good day; he had turned and once again gave me that same facial expression and never said a word to me. He got into his vehicle and took off, seconds later my dad pulled in and I was on my way home.

Not to mention, I was told by the psychiatrist that a report on the analysis of his evaluation of me would be ready in five days, and that I could pick up and submit it to my employer. The report was ready a couple of days before the Memorial Day holiday of '07!

I picked it up from his office, drove directly to City Hall and gave it to a union official that was very much familiar with my case from day one. Because of the doctor's attitude towards me, I did not open the envelope. His unprofessional attitude in his office at the end of my visit, I didn't want my holiday, Memorial Day having any clouds hanging over my head. But his light shines down on me. I'm a strong believer, that the truth is light! Thank you Jesus

My second son, is a member of The Class of 2007 at Oceanside Charter School. They had their Graduation Day, on Tuesday, June 12th, at 10 a.m. at the Holiday Inn, located in the beach block on Chelsea Avenue, in Atlantic City. Chris started at Oceanside in September of 2001, where he entered the third grade, and five years later graduated. He was given a plaque for his entire enrollment having great character! He never got suspended and stayed out of trouble while attending Oceanside Charter School. Chris and I were given a standing ovation for a job well done! Just think, what the City accused me of and being I'm a single parent and having such great children!

Chris was to have his orientation for summer employment with the City. The program was to run the beginning of July to third week of August. I informed him, there will be no need for him to participate in that program! "When someone tries to harm you, stay away from them." My daughter never took part in any school programs or community project for young girls in reaching maturity. It was called Rights of Passage. She seemed very interested in being a participant.

The PAL Center is named after a retired police sergeant, and the two of us have a bond. Mr. Scope along with my Dad, were Community Style Police Officers, always involved on some level with people or their children in the community. Both now retired men (Police Officers) were the coaches of two of the five Little League, Uptown baseball teams. Hackneys and Canada Dry were two teams, Mr. Scope (Hackneys) and Dad (Canada Dry). So I could realize what they would be missing not participating in those programs, but they will realize the power in Jesus.

My sons that summer both were working at the Surf Sandcastle Baseball Stadium located a few blocks from the Albany Avenue Bridge, a.k.a. "Peter F. Egnor Memorial Bridge". The work was steady for the both of them that summer, but one night, I had gone to pick them up after an evening/night game. I came across "H.N.I.C", who was working extra duty providing traffic and security. He noticed me sitting in my van and I noticed him as he walked by going to a traffic post. My sons came out and we headed for home. The next thing they cut their hours from working. My oldest son resigned because of his physical size, he felt they had him doing more, when others weren't pulling their weight. My youngest son continued to work when needed they called him to come in to work. I went to pick him up one night after he called! As I was heading over the Peter Egnor Memorial Bridge, I was at the same location on the memorial bridge when fireworks were displayed at the end of that game. It was a total surprise; it shook me up. I drove over the double yellow line, under Jesus' protection, no traffic was heading in the opposite direction. If so, it would have been a head on collision. I stopped on the bridge and called on Jesus shaking with tears coming out of my eyes. Moments later, I continued and picked up my son, Chris. When he entered the mini-van, he realized something had happened because I was visibly upset. I got control of myself and explained what had just happened. "Dad don't worry, I'm not working anymore at this stadium. Jesus, "will find a way, for us to make ends meet I have faith in Him." The stadium went out of business, shortly afterwards closing its doors for public entertainment.

I had to find a doctor that my insurance would cover for a fair evaluation. All I want is the truth from whomever the doctor may be. I searched around. I paid twenty-five dollars out of my pocket to speak with a doctor. He stated to me that the city doctor is unfit for the job and his contract was about to expire with the city. No one in their profession was willing to bid on the contract. I asked him why? He felt this doctor had caused more harm to people than he had ever helped. You would have double the workload to clean up his mess. It was just not worth it to him to bid on that City contract! This was not the only negative talk mentioned about this psychiatrist, he was in need of help himself. I finally found a doctor that my insurance would cover; I just wanted someone to be fair. They didn't have to agree with me, just be fair! I didn't have a problem when the City hired me on April 4th, 1994 and if they claim I have one now, take care of it!

They just don't realize who is large and really in charge! I was said to have Post-Trauma-Shooting. The only treatment available to me was medication and six to eight weeks' observation through counseling. I refused any type of medication to be given to me. The doctor I had chosen gave me some questioners and this was the result. He later learned I was supposed to have counseling only. Knowing Jesus, was all in charge, why worry! The Levy Administration changes because the Mayor was missing in action for about two weeks. Levy eventually stepped down from office. He was hiding out at a Rehab, a place I had been to before. He said he suffers from Post-Trauma-Shooting, because of the Vietnam War. He told people he was a Green Beret, which was far from the truth!

It was stated a new policy would be developed dealing with situation such as mine, a procedure that keep supervisors and their bosses or department head accountable for their actions taken toward an employee.

The whole Levy Administration was fired, and now they are out of work. "I wonder why?" I thank Jesus Christ, for what He had done, and what He is going to do, in my life! I will always keep Him first and carry Him with me regardless of my surrounding! The political process had become even more intertwined. The council President, another line Brother, became temporarily acting Mayor until another person was selected to finish out Mr. Levy's term which was the remaining two years.

The Democratic Committee, serving Atlantic City selected Ivan Scott - a high ranking fire official with the Atlantic City Fire Department to become the Mayor of Atlantic City. Of course, the horse and pony show really had its take off!

This Mayor was not the choice of the voting public, but of a committee. He would only serve one year in office, until the voting public would vote to place someone in for the remaining year left of the Levy Administration. Mayor "Langford," was voted back in as Mayor for that one year!

He ran again for the Democratic nomination in June and won! Now, he will run and mostly likely put out a win, being the Mayor who can turn the page and put Atlantic City back on its right track, from a City that has been a joke, into something more positive.

We all can turn the page, and move forward. Just like most Cities in our country needing help, Atlantic City is no different! Wards one thru four must realize, if the ship that we are in sinks, no matter where we position ourselves on the ship, we all will get wet, by our inconsiderate self-destruction of me and mine only mentally!

If you go out of your way to cause harm intentionally to someone, remember, what goes around, comes around in life! It may not catch you directly, but possibly someone near or dear to you! Feeling hurt or down, there be nothing that you can do, but pray. I put it in Jesus' hands! Protecting those who have or carry His awesome faith, and letting others know, all power rest in His hands, not in theirs! Jesus is, "The King of Kings", The Lord of Lords!

Chapter Fifteen

"Who Would Ever Believe?"

Back at home with Dad, my children living in a place not my own, reflecting on all the bad choices and things I had made, realizing a need for strength to continue my journey. Attacks from the adversary had increase in my life, the community changing from what it was, to now, crabs in a basket!. Yes, I have taken some comfort in the many changes, because I have been wash in Jesus blood!

My oldest son was preparing to graduate in June only several months away. By me not working, I felt that little could be done, but if I had my job much more could have been achieved, for this very special milestone in my son life! On March 21st, 2008, a buddy of mine whom I had worked with at Showboat, wanted me to accompany him to a party at the Soldier's Home, on his birthday! I decided to go. It was a B.Y.O.B. (bring your own bottle); food was furnish! I met up with a friend unexpectedly that we had a strong relationship in high school and some college! Her co-workers (girlfriends) after two and a half years of her mourning, the lost of her husband, she took up their invitation to go out! Anyway we met up at the affair. I invited her over to my table; we ate, drank some wine, and talked about everything. A much deserve time, we both needed, and both of us had it right there in the Soldier's Home! Fifteen minutes, before it was closing time, her friends came looking for her, finding us enjoying one another's company! I walked them to their car parked around the corner.On my way back to my vehicle; I had to use the men's room. I tried to enter the building but was refused entry by a supervisor that I had known for many years! I had met him at the Mayor's home during the passing of the Mayor's daughter!

I was dressed in a suit, just wanting to use the men's room only yards away from the entrance, but he refused to let me in! The Post (Soldier's Home) is named after Kenneth Hawkins, same as my last name, but I was expected to relieve myself outside, according to this supervisor's actions.

I was in City Hall on some other business, when I stopped to pass a few words at one of the security officers, (retired Capt. of A.C.P.D.) station on the lobby first floor. He was talking with a well-known Pastor in our community, sitting at a table, located at an entrance checkpoint. The supervisor, from the Soldier's Home walked up to the table and started shaking the other two gentlemen's hands in an acknowledgement gesture. When he extended his hand to me, I politely told the other two gentlemen I would talk with them later! The expression on their face was a puzzling one. I told them I had a problem with him because he wouldn't let me use the restroom that night, but expected me to use the outdoors! His excuse was, there was a problem inside on another level and he didn't want anyone to reenter the building. "Negro Please!" Was on my mind and I left the lobby of City Hall.

About forty days later, there was a busted by an investigation that led to the Supervisor's arrest for selling drugs on duty and using his assigned City vehicle at the Soldier's Home! I asked for mercy on him! I hate to see anyone lose their source of income especially when it's beyond their control. I know that feeling, but I also know someone who sits high and reaches down low! In the beginning, my faith was as small as a mustard seed! But with all that I have been through and what's yet to come, mighty mountains of faith are with me.

After the election in June of that year, for democratic favor in the polls in November, a councilman of the second ward, once working in city welfare, was indicted for voter fraud, the second time being charged. The first time, he was cleared of all charges! When I lost my job at PAL, I was living in his ward. He knew I was a single parent trying to do all I could for my children, but he never picked up the phone, stopped by, or sent a message, asking "Wesley what is going on!" just to show some concern or support! The councilman would stop by at the PAL to check on his hip-hop crew often weekly. I know, the official knew, and so did my Jesus!

Slowly withdrawing from being active with my church, the death of a longtime member, some other members, having secret hidden agendas they made against me in dealing with my children, I have learned to "forgive them all", and have no hard feelings towards them! With some people being one way on Sunday, you must watch out during the remaining days of the week with some of these same people. They call themselves proud Christian members. Church is for sick people, sick of the worldly things. But when you have no clue, of what you have done or you call yourself keeping it hidden; guess what, not from JESUS! If one does not correct their actions Jesus will bring it to the light! This reinforces, take it to Jesus, He does all but fail!

The councilman, along with a Superior Court Judge, is members of where I raised my children from their early ages! Have mercy on them! This judge wouldn't allow me to have any contact with my daughter. I didn't know she was mine until she was the age of ten, when the DNA proved I am her father. I was told by the court, (order) I would pay child support and provide health insurance. The mother would let me know how she was doing in school by sending her report card in the mail. Having faith, some five years later, I now have joint custody along with her brother's father! The new sitting Judge, was impress, first time on the bench he has given joint custody to two men of a child! The World is changing! This person helped raise both of her children; my daughter is the oldest and his son. She married some other guy with a criminal problem that has served prison time in Indiana and New Jersey. Only Jesus made it possible. All my children are loved, respectful and oriented. I'm truly, a blessed man!

Over the years returning to Bungalow Park, my father took on the responsibility of feeding the birds, cats, dogs and squirrels. He said they bring him luck playing the lottery! I would pull up, in front of the house, driving his car when out of nowhere, birds, cats and the squirrel walking the pole wires come to greet me, thinking I was my father. It rubbed off on me. Now, I'm thinking I'm Noah-Ark! The next thing, I took in a cat, it reminded me of the one we had living with us in the courts, (public housing) and my three children, fell in love with it. The cat at my Dad's home had two sets of kittens - each time six in each litter. Her last litter, my dad decided it was time to get rid of them. I took them over to the Humane Society located on Route 30 across from Venice Park. They wanted me to pay two hundred forty dollars to take them of my hands. One adult mother, one adult male cat from her previous liter and five kitten that were about two months old, a total of seven cats! My dad insisted I return home with the cats.

About a week later, I received information where to take the cats for free, no charge in taking them off our hands. Pleasantville is where we had to go. It was a very hot day in August '09, my dad was again set for this mission. This time my dad, a mutual friend, and I made that trip to Pleasantville Humane Society just off Franklin Boulevard. Because of repaving, on Franklin Boulevard traffic was detour onto Main Street and traffic was backed-up.. The cats were placed in the trunk of the car seat pull down with the air conditioner blasting, cats running freely, in the trunk looking at me sitting in the back seat. The Society was closed, I wanted to leave the cats, but my dad suggested not to; so we didn't.

On the way back to A.C., I suggested to go by the house to get some food for them. Then up to the boardwalk at New Jersey Avenue. After trying to turn the cats over to an agency, I suggested taking them up to the Boardwalk and someone would take them. They would not run from you but come to you in a playing mode. My dad didn't want to do that! We drove up to the said location. Ed, my Dad and I pull up to a lot across from the Revel tallest casino that was under construction. There were vehicles parked, belonging to the workers, some most with out of state, car tags displayed.

My Dad popped the trunk open, Ed and I took the cats out the car, placed them near the Boardwalk, and walked back to the car to get the cat food. Keeping an eye on them, I was on both knees, shaking the cat food in some bowls when suddenly, a young white unknown female came running up to me, screaming "What are you doing?" several times. I was in a kneeling position when I looked up, and noticed that a crew of construction workers unloading some materials about five stories up had stopped and were looking down on us. I then stood up, noticing the people walking on the Boardwalk stop in their tracks paying attention to this out of control person. She whipped out a cell phone, making a call while stating "There are three black guys who are cursing at me, hurry up and get here!"

Moments later, another unidentified woman came running up out of nowhere, Stating, "what the f—k are you doing," saying it several times, as though she were addressing each one of us. I told everyone not to say a word! The police responded from the Boardwalk and city patrol units. We were asked for I.D. which was provided to the police. One female officer, asked how many cats were there, and I stated six, one adult and five kittens, the other was left at home because it took off hiding when we're gearing up for the journey. The officer then said to me, there are only a total of five; one must be under the boardwalk because I heard it. You better go under there and get it! I refused her suggestion, stating not one cat disappeared; they stayed together. I was not about to go under the Boardwalk, I know what happens when sweeps are made for the homeless living under the Boardwalk. You start to inch out of control from the insects you will pick-up on your clothes. Then another officer approached me stating that because I had the kittens in the trunk, it being very hot that day, one of the kittens was barely moving and I would be held responsible if it died! Oxygen was given, and she rush off with lights and siren taking it to the Humane Society on Absecon Boulevard. At this time, they loaded the cats in the Humane Society vehicle that was parked when we arrived. The two women who were so unprofessional, left and never identified themselves, from outset. I was trying to contact the agency for their help but instead, more problems developed.

This occurred a couple of days or so before, Michael Vick, was arrested for inhumane treatment of some dogs; it seems again I was being painted with that same brush. An hour later a different person came from the Humane Society to my address and retrieved one kitten and one cat from a previous litter. This woman was very professional, compared to the other that made a bad impression on their agency, with me.

A week later, I had two charges filed against me concerning the cats, which included abandonment and transporting in a <u>cure</u> and inhumane manner; the summonses were sent in the mail. I pleaded, not guilty! I received a public defendant because of my income. My Dad was truly upset with me.

I knew all along who had my back and I didn't worry. At the court hearing in front of a Judge who no longer sits on the bench After approximately sixteen years of service to the City heard the case.

The abandonment was thrown out because I was going to speak about bringing to the light, how I was approached. I was informed by my Dad, he accidentally stepped on one of the kittens, that one police officer (veterinarian) stated a kitten had problems breathing because of the heat in the trunk. If that_were_the case, it, should affect them all. Again they were in air-conditioning along with its passengers.

The Judge found me guilty, but again because I am one of Jesus' children I wasn't worried! I was fine, and had to perform community service for fifteen days, "no problem"! The community service I had an issued with, because I was not going to volunteer any service for that cleaning agency, feeding the animals and Mike Vick was on most racists' minds. The Judge and I got into a heated conversation about it. He finally ordered me to complete the service at City Hall. "A piece of cake", how sweet it was

During this time, I called the Hope Six program to see if they had any place where my family could move. Three years with my dad it was now time to move on, I love my Dad, but my Jesus does not fail and He may not be there when we wan him, but He is always . . . "Always right on time"!

I was told by the (Hope Six) how strange this was because they were going to send me a check, and take my name off their waiting list for a new home/housing.. They had shown me several other properties but I refused because of their locations. This time it was in the seven hundred block of Baltic Avenue. A few days later, I inspected the location and whole heartedly agreed, to set up to move in, the earliest six weeks later, "October" my move in date! My pension and social security disability kicked in! I was able to furnish my entire home with store bought furniture. I give God all the Glory and Praise!

At this time, please allow me to acknowledge that all four of my children graduated from Oceanside Charter School, then entered Atlantic City High as freshmen.

My youngest daughter graduated June 10th, 2009. She received two plaques for an outstanding job while attending Oceanside

Charter. First plaque, Longevity going there from the start of her education, 2001-2009. The second plaque, Technology Award, being up on her computer skills. I was a very proud Dad at her graduation! I lost my job trying to get the computer at home in working condition for my children. Mr. Undercover Supervisor-4-12 didn't play the music that year, as he has at many other children (sons') graduation in past years. One of the teachers, whom we both belonged to O.N.E Fraternity in high school, played the graduation march at the Soldier's Home, during the morning special event!!! Jesus, you get all the praises! Thank You for allowing me to press on, with "My Bridge Over Troubled Waters" a testimony on how awesome You are in my Life!

I now conclude my never ending Testimony in its final chapter of "Sweet Sixteen" Are you Ready!

Chapter Sweet Sixteen

"Over Approximately 30 Years, I Still Stand!"

Bringing my journey up to speed some twenty nine years later, all that goes on seems the tide has changed. Those who tried to affect me causing unjustified hardship to mine, it was their turn to be affected. The names of most that were listed on my suspension pending termination notification letter were on the chopping block to lose their positions. I'm not perfect and only human, so I pray for myself, for forgiveness, in having ill feelings towards those who tried to hurt me, affecting my children. Again all praises to Him!

The stress in the Police and Fire Departments as a whole is never discussed nor addressed unless it is in local newspapers resulting in arrests, or misconduct as a public official. These people, who are sworn into these roles, are chosen from society, with all its baggage.

I'm not surprised at the different allegations that have happened in the fire stations or dealing with our firemen.

The senseless death of several police officers by a self-destruction action. One may be told and you can believe what you want, there are quite a few who know better, of what was being said. They are lead to believe, that they are that "Super Hero" they can do fine, all by themselves? So far from the truth! On top of it all, get your personal relationship with your maker, if possible, fall on your knees, sit alone take some time out, ask for his protection, give forgiveness or whatever works for you, it's for you. Don't ever get up-set because someone appears to be doing better than you. You want what they got. But we don't know the price they paid in their walk with Jesus to be blessed by Him! What is yours, is for you only, no one else.

Since 911, accompany by routine duties every person should be evaluated at least three times during their career that they hold upon retirement. Even if there no red flags popping up this should including all ranks.The doctors who have contracts to deal with the mental stabilities of new or employee should be held accountable. Example, numerous Internal Affairs Complaints on attitudes on an individual, (officer) call out days, or treatment on injuries that happen, a pattern starts to develop. It should be "Nipped it in the Bud" by contracted medical staff. At a council meeting, the second ward official stated better lighting was being installed in the Back Maryland Marina District, because of the amount of shootings and criminal activities.

"Keeping it real!" People have been killed in broad day light, it can't any brighter than the Sun! So, if you are going to increase the wattage of light in that area of your ward, which also include some officers being taken from their desk jobs, to the front line, patrol!

I can understand Police not feeling safe, but think about those who live there and those who travel to get to work at the nearby casinos.

It is my humble opinion that lighting should be placed on the three public schools that seem to be dark, very low perimeter lighting. It could serve as a double fold purpose.

The first, showing younger school age children having light is bright for their educational future, as in everything, the truth comes to the light! Second, a possible deterrent in criminal activity around its surroundings, Uptown Park, Stanley Holmes Village, Westside Complex just to name a few places. Offshore schools are well lit at night! A person can be identified because of the lighting if it comes to going before a judge, from a complaint.

The entire country has fallen on a short fall on its operational budget, costing many to lose their jobs nationwide. Atlantic City is no different! Therefore, have faith! You, and your family will be alright. Stuff is placed on our shoulder, but with Faith, it will be handled.

If you are a problem person all along, don't be surprise when those problems, show back up. In some cases, they were there the whole entire time. Give thanks, for being alive, able to stay focused, love yourself by loving JESUS! This is just a test, of many tests that

163

will show up knocking at your door! You can handle it with His help! "Warning", it can't be done alone. Take the "S" off the chest, its ok you are human! Again it will be handled in His favor. Remember a plan has been made for each and every one of us from our first breath of air, we would not know a plan exsist keep the faith, He will see you through! A person who rebounds from a situation that tried to hold them down says a lot!

I have met law enforcement officers locally, across this State and country over the past thirty years. Although I only spent eight years, one month and two day as a sworn police officer, the blessing is in having my dad, who been retired since 1983 from A.C.P.D. who is still with me as I walk this Journey!

Some officers stated because of my actions on that bridge, they don't have to ever worry about that individual ever confronting them on the streets. He's a done deal! I save the taxpayers of New Jersey, not having to give him room and board in Trenton State Prison for the rest of his life. Although I'm not receiving what I was entitled to with the post-tram, as a police officer but instead on a security guard salary, rather my policemen salary doing that time of my resignation. Knowing who is large and in charge of my life and it's not me, I press on each and every day, as 30 years will soon to come, still standing, and mentally truly bless!

A friend who was a bit older, whose brother is the same age as I, all growing up in Bungalow Park, was accidentally killed on his job site by electrocution working at a school. He was a certified electrician. On the day of his funeral which was held at a Catholic church on North Pennsylvania Avenue, the line paying your final respects was long. About forty people were standing in line waiting on entering the church. I was walking to the end of the line, when the former Chief of police who stepped down, under the current administration, he was no longer in charge of the daily operation of the police department. He had to report/answer to a female boss, the new Public Safety Director. Him being from the "good ole boy" network that is still around, in my opinion like racism, we met at the end of the line. He stood behind me in line.

Not once did we pass a greeting to one another! Some of his friends were speaking to him that had formed outside the church. Hey chief, how we miss your presence. He said to them, "Don't worry, they are going to get it for what they did to me"! I said to myself, you and your network tried to do me, from day one but I ask for mercy to you all! "What goes around comes around!"

Standing at the entrance about to enter the church, the former Mayor, now a State Senator representing our District got out of line, walked over to me, shook my hand, and exchanged some small talk. Standing behind me talking with others as we waited to enter, the former chief was on top of his game with his well-wishers! I was wondering, not questioning, why would Jesus, put me here standing in front of this individual, with all his fanfare. As we entered the church, I took out my ink pen and signed my name in the family book of attendance. I then turned offering my ink pen for the

165

former chief to use. At that very moment, the tide change people were now asking me how I was doing, my children and Dad! Most were people from Bungalow Park that we all grew up together that I hadn't seen in years.

After viewing my friend, I approached the family who was standing just off from their family departed member; I spoke with his sister, letting her know who I was. Also saying one day, I will join her club, smiling! Next was her youngest brother, he was looking downward with no facial expression on his face. I said Don Don, remember me, Wesley! He started looking upward slowly saying my name when we made eye contact, he gave me a friendly embracement shouting my name. His brother in-law asks us to allow the line to move on and we did. I'm glad I brought a smile to his face and one in the heart. We serve an awesome Jesus Christ! These last few years, approaching the thirty year anniversary of my partner's death and stepping on with faith, many decades ago a mustard seed was planted in my life. To be able to still stand, again I give JESUS all the entire Glory!

My relationship with someone who will always hold a special place in my heart, had taken me under her wing. I guess, I seemed lost because of not participating in my church activities, in which I once had. A few members passing on, in which they had a strong hold onto my family and me in church activities. Reaching out to my Pastor, his wife who I respect and love dearly, we lost our connection, in dealing, with my family.in which we had for years. Some members seemed to have some consideration on my well-being as a single parent. The person who spread this rumor that resulted in my losing my job at PAL is also a member of the church. I can only pray for them! You don't have to worry about me or mine ever entering those doors at the PAL Center for anything, ever! It's sad, those at that P.A.L Center because of their ego or whatever, stained that center like J. Edgar Hoover did the F.B.I. Building in Washington D.C.; I continue to pray.

I have visited some churches during my absent from Second Baptist my home church. After several attempts made to get my Pastor to bless our new home, he was never able to for fill my request.. Yes, Jesus was still working in our lives. One evening while exiting a store, next to the Community Baptist Church, the new Pastor, I invited him to please, come to bless our home. He promised he would. Within an hour my door bell rang, to my surprise accompanied with one of his deacons, my request was filled. He was also a former member of Second Baptist Church, now a Pastor.

Looking outside from my front door across the street is New Hope Church, whom the Pastor, I have known a many of years! He can break the word down, so you can understand, place it in your heart and keep it on your mind throughout your journey in life! The Learning Center, belonging to "New Hope" Baptist Church, opens to any preschool youth. I believe the purple and gold activity play set and the church name alone reflects an interest in my life. What a location, for me a mustard seed planted close to thirty years ago about to harvest.

The most important thing about being knocked down is getting back up! It can be done; don't give up, keep the faith!

On my Birthday, I plan to join The New Shiloh Baptist Church just up the street; it's also in walking distant. The Bishop James Washington is real, I can relate to him. Where everyone is welcome! No one sits on a thrown, not even Bishop! He has that "southern personality" and can sing, that leads me into toe tapping, head bobbing and hands clapping spirit. Bishop, preaches the word straight from the Holy Bible! It made me want to get involved with the church, where others who I know, may seem to find their fulfillment, to a void that's can be most difficult to be fill. An inner search of themselves may be found at New Shiloh. A person blessing is their blessing, we don't know what they went through to get what they got in their blessings. We serve an awesome Master, if you believe in Him! I will always hold on to His hand, for He has brought me a long way, eventually and eternally being among Him in His promise land!

On October 14th, 2010, at 8 a.m., standing with many on the Peter F. Egnor Memorial Bridge, breezy quite Sun fills morning. Services for the laying of the reef for my partner, who paid the ultimate, his life. A new Police Commander, Deputy Chief Jubilee who was in charge of the brief ceremony spoke to those that were present.

The first time in 29 years, ever that I had saw a Mayor in or out of office attend the ceremony! He was accompanied by the Public Safety Director..

Also, I was mention of being present and was in the patrol car sitting next to Pete.. We didn't have the opportunity to speak, but I know my partner was smiling down on me saying, "Yo Man, the best is yet to come,!" I stand on Faith, on "My Bridge Over Troubled Waters," giving Jesus, all the Glory, for all that He's done and all that He will do in my journey of life!

One year later, on the 30th Anniversary of my partner's death, on the bridge, I was asked to take part in memorial ceremony, by giving a reef to his family to be placed at his gravesite! Also, my father had driven to the ceremony at least three times over the thirty years. He would stay in the car, normally parked along with other vehicles at the foot of the bridge. I asked him why he never came to the ceremony. He revealed to me, "the whole situation was handled incorrectly!" When those shots first rang out, someone should have had those units back down, and had a roadblocks set up on route 40? Not to mention "what they tried" to take you through! But look, they think they gave me opportunity some thirty years later, to express myself, but it was nobody but Jesus, from day one! Yes, having Dad with me on the 30th standing next to me was awesome; yes the best has yet to come!

I thank all persons for your support and patience you provided to me in writing this book! I wanted it completed a year or so ago.

Remember, it's not what you want, but instead what Jesus wants you to have! This Testimony is Jesus, how he works in my life. I pray that this book touches so many of His People! If our paths ever cross on this highway of life, feel free to share some moments because the best has yet to come, "My Bridge over Trouble Waters"!

RESPECTFULLY

WESLEY HAWKINS, JR.

2014

Snapshots of my past...

Self 1957   Mom & Dad

MIL ACAD CHOIR   SIS GRAD DETROIT 1971

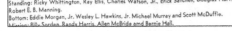

ONE FRAT 1975

Year Book Staff

July 15, 1979, Sworn In As Acpd

Partner's burial

Wes Jr.

33rd Session of ACPA Graduating Class
July 11, 1980

Wes Sr. Last Day - Retirement

OPP Line Brothers & First
Black Mayor AC

Bro Rbt Medly & Wife @
Delta Que Ball

Delta Que Ball

In Patrol Car Pic By Pete Egnor

Detective Buear
after an arrest

Casino Security

Self and Que Bro
Henry Charles

Children First Night with Dad

Christmas

Easter

Christmas years later

Wes III Oceanside Graduation

Team Players - AC Wealfare

SBC Rev Sharpton and Wes Jr

TJMS Taj Mahal Casino

Chris Graduation & Frat Bro's

Dr MLK Always

Headstart Teacher & Miriah

Wes III
The Fisherman

Wes III Oceanside Grad Party

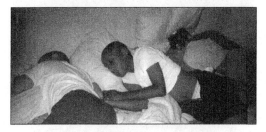

Jesus Has Us!

The Hawkins Boys

Mother & Grandmother

Christopher Livin Large

Dad & Pedro his partner

Omega Family Picnic 2009

Then

Then

Only a Rose Cotillion

Now

Now   Standing

Family in tow, with Christ   Chief Jubilee, my father and I

Still Standing

30th Anniversary of partner's death

30th Anniversary on the Bridge

I pray that my auto-biography touches so many of his people . . . .even those person who are unaware of his work. Please feel free to share . . . this book with friends, some co-workers . . .those connected to law enforcement current or retire officers. Yes. . .the best has yet to come in "My Bridge Over Trouble Waters".

Enclosing I would love my favorite scripture that I can say had a everlasting whole on me for start to finish of my book & also the steps that I took, along my journey.

Proverbs . . . . Chapter 3 . . .verses 5 &6! (5) "Trust in the Lord with all thine heart; and lean not unto thine own understanding." (6) "In all thy ways acknowledge him, and he will shall direct thy paths." Thank you all and I give my praises to Jesus **the Christ, for directing me, to give my testimony in what he has done for me in my** life, when I did not have him or myself. . .**now we have each other, never to part ever again.**

Sincerely, respectfully yours

Wesley Hawkins Jr.

2014

CPSIA information can be obtained at www.ICGtesting.com
Printed in the USA
BVOW06s2135131115

426865BV00004B/4/P

9 781629 526478